Yeshua, the Firstborn Word/Wisdom

Copyright 2020 by Shmuel Playfair
© TXu 2-190-539

Our Fathers Inherited Lies

In Jeremiah 16.19-20, we read, "Nations (גּוֹיִם *Goyeem*) will come to You (*HaShem* י-ה-ו-ה) from the ends of the earth and say, 'Certainly our ancestors/fathers inherited falsehood, worthless futility in which there is no benefit/purpose.'" Unfortunately, Christians today do not realize they have inherited worthless falsehood, so they teach and pass on futile lies, which they mistakenly believe to be the truth.

Most lies found in today's mainstream Christianity were established by non-Jewish Church fathers at various councils, including Constantine's famous Council of Nicea in 325 C.E. Jews who understood and upheld the original Hebrew/Jewish Scriptures were not invited to this assembly, which replaced Yeshua, the biological Jewish son/descendant of David, with a virgin-born "Jesus," a pagan god-man. Furthermore, the anti-Jewish theologians replaced the single infinite Creator Who has no equals with a foreign Threesome deity in which the imaginary god-man, "Jesus," is one of three distinct co-equal, co-eternal god-persons who were co-Creators.

As Constantine's deceptive Christianity evolved, its leaders further claimed that their plural deity instituted a brand-new covenant for everyone with brand new laws apart from the Instruction/*Torah*/Law of Moses. For example, they rejected the need for a renewal of the original covenant relationship with the single Creator through repentance and subsequent faithful obedience to His Instruction/Law. As anti-*Torah*/Law teachers, they also advocated a foreign belief in a vicarious or substitutionary atonement for sin by their god-man's human sacrifice, which negated the need for individuals to take responsibility to make atonement for their sins as taught in the Jewish Scriptures.

Pagan Christian theologians taught as well that their imaginary god-man, Jesus, fulfilled the Law of Moses and thereby ended it by nailing it to the cross at the time of his death. In this way, he terminated his followers' need to keep the *Torah*/Law given to God's people. Consequently, the false God-man, the lawless anti-Christ, allegedly freed people from God's Instruction/Law and gave them a license to do such things as to eat formerly forbidden foods, including pork and shellfish.

Constantine's Christianity further cut ties with *HaShem*'s *Torah*/Instruction by rejecting *Torah* observances such as keeping the *Shabbath* Day holy, *Yom T'ruah* (the Day of the *Shofar* Blast), *Yom Kippur*, *Sukkot*, and Passover. Additionally, this anti-*Torah* religious movement *replaced* the Creator's seventh day of rest (*Shabbath*) with the celebration of the weekly Sun's day and incorporated pagan Easter worship at the Spring equinox in place of the annual Passover festival of Unleavened Bread. Constantinian Christianity also established the sun god's birthday on December 25th as a day to honor the birthday of its fabricated god-man.

In the preface to Edward Gibbon's book, <u>History of Christianity</u>, we read: "If Paganism was conquered by Christianity, it is equally true that Christianity was corrupted by Paganism." [p. xvi] This reconciliation or union of opposing principles and practices is called "religious syncretism." In the following seven volumes/books, I will use the *TaNaKh* (the Hebrew Scriptures) and the Renewed Covenant Scriptures written by Jews to identify and refute many non-*Torah* falsehoods promoted by the pagan Church Fathers and their followers today.

(Volume One)
One God, the Father/Creator
"יָ-ה-וּ-ה Alone!"

(Volume Two)
One Human Master: Yeshua's Identity in the Jewish Scriptures

(Volume Three)
Five Important Aspects of Yeshua's Jewish Identity

ONE: Yeshua, the Firstborn Word/Wisdom

TWO: Yeshua, the Patrilineal Son of David

THREE: Yeshua, the Servant of *HaShem*

FOUR: Yeshua, the Messiah "*Ben*" *Yoseph*

FIVE: "Jesus," the Counterfeit Christ Versus Yeshua, the Genuine Messiah

(Volume Four)
HaShem's Covenant and
His *Torah*/Law

(Volume Five)

Repentance, Sacrifice, and
Redemption

(Volume Six)

Who is a "Jew" or an "Israelite"?

(Volume Seven)

Interpreting the *TaNaKh*;
Interpreting Yeshua; Interpreting
Paul; Answering Objections;
Responses to Christian Anti-Judaism

Yeshua, the Firstborn Wisdom/Word

Table of Contents

Acronyms and Terms

Adonai (אֲדֹנָי) means "my great MASTER/LORD" and is often used as a Hebrew circumlocution for the Creator's name

Ayn Sof (a reference to God as the One without end)

a.k.a. (also known as)

BDB (a Hebrew and English Lexicon of the Old Testament by Brown, Driver, Briggs)

C.E. (Common Era)

cf. (the abbreviation in Latin for *confer/conferatur* meaning "compare")

DSS (Dead Sea Scrolls)

Eloheem/Elohim (a Hebrew title meaning "Powerful Sovereign" usually translated as "God" in English)

HaShem (a Hebrew word meaning "the Name," which refers to the name (י-ה-ו-ה) of the Creator found throughout the Hebrew Scriptures)

J.W. (Jehovah Witnesses)

LXX (Septuagint)

Midrash (the Hebrew term "*Midrash*" comes from the root word, *darash* דרש, which means to seek, to search out, or to dig for meaning. "Midrash' is the haggadic or halachic exposition or mode of biblical/textual interpretation employed by ancient Judaic authorities)

Midrash Rabbah (meaning "Great Midrash") can refer to part of or the collective whole of specific aggadic *midrasheem* on the books of the *Torah* and the Five *Megillot*

MT (Masoretic Text)

NT (New Testament = Renewed Covenant Scriptures)

NAS/NASB (the New American Standard Bible)

NRSV (the New Revised Standard Version)

OT (Old Testament)

RaDaK (Rabbi David Kimchi, 1160 – 1235)

RaMBaM (*Rabbi Moshe ben Maimon/Maimonides*, 1135 – 1204)

TaNaKh (an acronym for *Torah* (תּוֹרָה), meaning Instruction or Teaching; *N'vee'eem* (נְבִיאִים), meaning Prophets; and (כתובים), meaning Writings

Talmud (Instruction, learning from the Hebrew root "*lmd*" teach/study) These important texts of Rabbinic Judaism are also referred to as "*ShaS*," which is a Hebrew abbreviation of '*Sheesha Sedareem*" meaning the "six orders." It usually refers to the Babylonian Talmud rather than the Jerusalem Talmud.

Targum (an Aramaic translation or paraphrase of the Hebrew Scriptures

YHWH or ***YHVH*** (two popular English transliterations for the Hebrew letters of the Hebrew name of the Creator)

List of Abbreviations for Philo's Works

   Agr. or Agric. (De Agricultura/On Agriculture)

   Confl. or Conf. Ling. (De Confusione Linguarum)

   Det. (Quod Deterius Potiori Insidiari Soleat)

   Ebr. (De Ebrietate/On Drunkenness)

   Fug. (De Fuga et Invention)

   Her. or Heres (Quis Rerum Divinarum Heres Sit)

   Leg. All. (Legum Allegoriarum)

   Migr. (De Migratione Abrahami)

   Sacr. AC. (De Sacrificiis Abelis et Caini)

   Som. (De Sommiis/On Dreams)

   Qu. Gen. (Quaestiones et Solutiones in Genesin)

Different Print Types

The bold print represents the author's thoughts/words.

Individual *italicized* words are used either for emphasis or to indicate the English transliteration of Hebrew, Aramaic, or Greek words.

Bold print all in italics represents someone else's thoughts/words with which the author agrees.

The regular print is another person's thoughts/words with which the author usually disagrees. [One may choose to skip parts of the regular print in order to read more quickly.]

FOREWORD

The purpose of this book is to serve as a resource for those who seek to correctly understand what the Jewish Scriptures teach regarding a controversial theological issue. Instead of reading the whole body of material straight through, some may prefer to focus on specific topics of interest. Readers should keep in mind that repetitive arguments help reinforce an accurate interpretation of the Jewish Scriptures.

I especially want to thank my loving wife and best friend, Carolyn Cable Playfair, for her assistance with editing this book.

"In the beginning was the Word, and the Word was with the (Most High Creator) God/Power, and the Word was 'God/Power' … And the Word became flesh…." [John 1.1-18]

Introductions: The Unborn/Uncreated Father/Creator and His Firstborn, First-Created Word/Wisdom

It should be noted that God's first-created personified Word was the vocal expression of God's Wisdom, which was both the means/instrument of His creation and His revealed Instruction/Law given to His people. In the beginning, the single Creator created or gave birth to the personified "firstborn" Word/Wisdom or Instruction/Law.

Furthermore, the single Creator/Source created all things through/by means of the personified Word/Wisdom. John pictures the spoken personified Word/Wisdom (*not* the Creator Himself) as much later becoming embodied in the life, works, and teachings of a historical human being, Yeshua. No human being has ever physically seen God, the invisible immortal Father/Creator. However, the visible, mortal, and faithfully obedient son, Yeshua, the one being in the bosom (i.e., who lives in harmony with the will) of the Father--that one explained or made the Creator known. [cf. John 1.1-18]

In stark contrast to a threesome God with three distinct god-persons imagined by the pagan church fathers, Paul writes in 1 Corinthians 8.6, "Yet for us, there is one (single) God, the Father/Creator, *from* Whom are all things....and one Master/Lord *through* whom are all things." "*Through* whom are all things" refers to the personified firstborn first-created Word/Wisdom embodied in the life and teachings of Yeshua. Because the (spoken) Word/Wisdom is the instrument or means *through* which God, the Father/Creator created all things, it can*not* simultaneously be the single Creator, the Originator, or the Source of all creation. Unfortunately, misguided idolaters mistakenly equate the "firstborn (Word/Wisdom) *of* creation" with the single Creator Who is neither "born" nor "*of* creation."

Note that Paul, John, and other writers of the Renewed Covenant Scriptures distinguish "the From Whom Are All Things" (the only Most High God, the Father/Creator) from the "through whom are all things" (the firstborn of creation" the personified, firstborn first-created Word/Wisdom). Since the later historical human creature, Yeshua, embodied the spoken personified Word/Wisdom in his life and teachings, he is figuratively called the beginning of the Creator's works or acts of creation, *through* or *by* whom the single God created all things. [cf. Rev. 3.14] At the same time, Paul, John, and the other Jewish writers acknowledge the Father/Creator as the one and only Ultimate Power, *the* Most High God, and distinguish Him from the firstborn, first-created Word/Wisdom, which functions as the Father/Creator's subservient instrument/means.

Paul, John, and the other writers Renewed Covenant Scriptures never claim that the first-created, firstborn born Word/Wisdom *of* the creation "at the beginning" is "as eternal as God is." That false idea was made up later by pagan church fathers who equated the human Yeshua who embodied the (spoken) Word/Wisdom in his life and teachings with his Father/Creator. Only the unborn Creator Who has no beginning is eternal and uncreated.

Paul teaches in 1 Timothy 2.5, "For there is one (single) God (the Father/Creator) and one mediator between God and humanity, a *man* (not a God>man), Messiah Yeshua." Many have yet to acknowledge or accept Paul's statement of faith, "But, for us, there is one God, the Father...." Instead, these people claim that "...for us there is one threesome God: the father plus the son plus the spirit...."

The Firstborn Wisdom/Word Personified

According to dictionary.com, "to personify" means "to attribute human nature or character to an inanimate object or an abstraction." So, a "personification" refers to 1) "the attribution of human characteristics to things, abstract ideas, et cetera, for literary or artistic effect or 2) the representation of an abstract quality or idea in the form of a person, creature, et cetera, as in art and literature. Thus, when someone personifies an object or abstraction, one describes something which is not a real person *as if* it was a human person.

For example, in Proverbs eight, the author talks about God's wisdom as if it was a female person. This personification does not mean that God's wisdom was a literal physical woman of flesh and blood. Instead, the author pictures the abstract idea of God's wisdom as a female entity. The Jewish wisdom writer does not mean that the Creator's wisdom was an actual human person.

Beginning with the author of Proverbs eight and continuing with others like Joshua *ben Sira*, Philo, and later John, Jewish wisdom writers picture the non-human abstractions of the Creator's "wisdom" and later His "word" *as if* it is a human person. These writers understood that "wisdom" and "word" are abstract concepts and not actual human beings. So, keep in mind that for Jewish wisdom writers, the "personification" of abstractions such as "wisdom" and "word" are not referencing an actual historical human being. In other words, the personified "Word" embodied in Yeshua's life and teachings, which was present at creation, was not a real, physical human creature at the beginning of creation.

Note that a generation before Yeshua, Philo refers to Moses, a real historical human creature, as being "the law-giving Word." [Migr. 23f; cf. 122] Later, John pictures Yeshua, another historical human person, as "the Word made flesh." [John 1.1-14] In other words, both Philo and John employ personification to portray the abstract word/wisdom of the Creator as becoming embodied in the life and teachings of two actual historical human creatures, Moses and Yeshua. Neither Moses nor Yeshua, the son of Joseph and Miriam, were physically present at creation but rather lived much later in human history.
https://www.facebook.com/martin.stivala.3/posts/183880666 9565311

The Five Characteristics of the Firstborn Word/Wisdom Listed in Colossians 1.15-17

In the Renewed Covenant Scriptures, the Jewish authors portray Yeshua as being each one of four different categories of "firstborn." While these four distinct types of "firstborn" are related to each other, they should not be mixed up or conflated:

A) According to Psalm 89.27-29, *HaShem* appointed His anointed king (initially David and ultimately his biological descendant, Yeshua) as His *"firstborn, supreme over the kings of the earth."*

B) In Romans 8.29, Paul refers to Yeshua as *"the firstborn (son) among many siblings."* [cf. Heb. 12.23]

C) In Colossians 1.18, due to God resurrecting Yeshua from the dead, Paul portrays Yeshua as being *"…the firstborn from the dead* so that he might become first in everything."

D) Additionally, in Colossians 1.15-17, Paul lists the following five characteristics of the firstborn Word/Wisdom, which he applies metaphorically to Messiah Yeshua:

 1) the image of the invisible God, [Colossians 1.15]
 2) *the firstborn of all creation.* [Colossians 1.15; cf. John 1.1]
 3) …all things in the heavens and on the earth were created in/because of him, the visible, and the invisible…all things were created through/by means of him and for him. [Colossians 1.16; cf. John 1.3; 1 Corinthians 8.6]
 4) He is *before* (*pro* πρò) all things, [Colossians 1.17; cf. John 1.2] and
 5) In him, all things hold together. [Colossians 1.17]

While it is helpful to distinguish the four categories of "firstborn," it is especially important to understand the significance of the five characteristics of the firstborn Word/Wisdom, which Paul applies metaphorically to Yeshua in Colossians 1.15-17. Unfortunately, Paul's application of five characteristics of the firstborn Word/Wisdom to Yeshua is often interpreted literally rather than metaphorically. Consequently, many today mistakenly suppose that referring to the historical Yeshua as "the firstborn *of* creation," means that he pre-existed as a visible human person or as an individual human spirit before the world was made.

Most people are not aware that Renewed Covenant writers like John and Paul were influenced by Jewish Wisdom literature when they identified Yeshua metaphorically as the Creator's personified Wisdom/Word. For example, a generation before Yeshua was born, Philo, a prolific wisdom writer, pictured Abraham as "the model of Wisdom" and depicted Moses as "the Law-giving Word." [On Dreams 1. 69-70; Migr. 23.; cf. 122] In a similar manner, John later described Yeshua as "the Word become flesh." [John 1.14] And, Paul portrayed Yeshua as the embodiment of *HaShem*'s firstborn Word/Wisdom. The effect of various Jewish Wisdom writers on Paul's writings is especially evident in Colossians 1.15-17, where Paul applied the following five characteristics or attributes of the firstborn Word/Wisdom metaphorically to Yeshua:

1) "the image of the invisible God"
In Jewish Wisdom literature, God's firstborn personified Word/Wisdom is considered to be the image (plan/design) of the invisible God, the Father/Creator. For example, God's first-created Wisdom is referred to as being "the image of God" in Wisdom 7.26 and in Philo's *Legum Allegoriae* 1.43. So, also, Philo speaks of God's disclosed *Logos* (Word) as being "the image of God" in *De confusione linguarum* 97, 147; *De Fuga et inventione* 101; *De somnis* 1.239; 2.45. Later, in Colossians 1.15, Paul characterizes Yeshua, who embodied the (spoken) Word/Wisdom in his

life and teaching, metaphorically, as "the image of the invisible God."

2) "the firstborn *of* all creation"

One should understand that in the Jewish Scriptures the Hebrew term for "firstborn," "*b'khor*" (בְּכֹר), along with its Greek equivalent, "*prototokos*" (πρωτότοκος), refers primarily to "one who first opens the womb" or "one born first." In Hebrew/Jewish culture, the son "born first" (in terms of time) secondarily carries an important implication for the laws of inheritance. So, the "firstborn (son)," a "*b'khor*" (בְּכֹר) or a "*prototokos*" (πρωτότοκος), is born first both in terms of time and rank. Likewise, the personified Word/Wisdom is firstborn of the created order both in terms of time and rank.

Additionally, the full Greek phrase Paul uses in Colossians 1.15, "*prototokos pasas ktiseos* (πρωτότοκος πάσης κτίσεως)," is correctly translated as "the firstborn *of* all creation." No Greek preposition or adjective meaning or indicating "*over*" is found here. Nevertheless, some translators prefer to say, "the firstborn *over* all creation" because they want to support their false propaganda that Yeshua is one of three different co-equal, co-eternal god-persons, none of whom are actually "*of* creation." However, just as the firstborn son of a family" is a member of the family, so also, "the firstborn of creation" (Yeshua) is a member of creation. Again, misguided interpreters insist on using the non-existent preposition "over" all God's creation when translating Colossians 1.15 in order to avoid the truth that the "firstborn" son is part *of* (i.e., belongs to) God's creation.

Throughout Jewish Wisdom literature, the personified Word/Wisdom is portrayed as being "the firstborn *of* all creation" who was with, beside, or next to (*pros* πρὸς = אֵצֶל

etzel) its Creator in the beginning *before* the physical world is created. As we read in Proverbs 8.22-31, "י-ה-ו-ה (*HaShem*) brought me (Wisdom) forth, created or acquired me (*kananee* קְנָנִי, which is a poetic use of the verb *kanah* קָנָה meaning "acquired") at the beginning of His way, before His deeds from of old. From time immemorial, I was appointed from the beginning of the world. When there were no oceans, I was given birth when there were no springs abounding water. Before the mountains were settled [in place], before the hills, I was born... Then I was a craftsman [*amon* אָמוֹן = marksman] beside (next to) Him (the single Creator). Moreover, I was delighting day by day rejoicing before Him (in *HaShem*'s presence) all of the time." [cf. John 1.1-3] Also, Philo pictures God's revealed Wisdom as being "the *first* of all God's works" (Prov. 8.22), and he refers to God's disclosed *Logos* (Word) as "the eldest *of* created things." [*Leg. All.* III.175] Later in Colossians 1.15, Paul characterizes Yeshua metaphorically as "the firstborn *of* all creation" (both in time and rank) because he embodied the firstborn Word/Wisdom in his life and teachings.

 3) "all things were created in and through him"

In Jewish Wisdom literature, *HaShem*'s revealed Word/Wisdom is considered to be not only brought forth or created by God (Proverbs 8.22; Sirach 1.4; 24.9), but also as an instrument, means, or agency by/through which God (the sole Father/Creator) created all things. [see Proverbs 3.19; Wisdom 8.4-6; Philo in *Det.* 54] In other words, during creation, God spoke/commanded first, then various aspects of the physical universe fulfilled His word or command. As we read in Genesis 1.3, "God *said*, 'Be light'…And it was so." Consequently, because Yeshua embodied the (spoken) Word/Wisdom in his life and teachings, in Colossians 1.16, Paul portrays Yeshua metaphorically as the one "in/because of whom were created all things in the heavens and on the earth, the visible and the invisible…"

4) "he is before ("*pro* πρò) all things"

Jewish Wisdom literature personifies God's firstborn Word/Wisdom as the one "*HaShem* (ה-ו-ה-י) brought forth/possessed" (*kanani* קָנָנִי) at the *beginning* of His way. It is the one whom *HaShem* "appointed, installed, set up from the beginning" or the one who "was given birth when there were no oceans…." [cf. Prov. 8.22-31] [By the way, "brought forth" or "possessed" (*kanani* קָנָנִי)" is the verb which Eve used in Genesis 4.1 to describe the birth of her firstborn son, Cain.]

Note that in Sirach 1.4, we read, "Wisdom was created *before* all things." And the Jewish philosopher Aristobulus (who lived in the second century BCE) writes that "Wisdom existed *before* heaven and earth." [Eusebius, *Praeparatio Evangelica* 13.12.11] In this regard, John 1.1-3 speaks of the personified *Logos* (Word) being beside/next to its Creator "in the beginning" meaning *before* everything else was created. In other words, according to the original account of the creation recorded in Genesis along with the later Jewish Wisdom literature, God spoke, brought forth, birthed, or created His Word/Wisdom first, and then the rest of creation followed.

Note that the Greek preposition, "*pro* (πρò)," which Paul uses in Colossians 1.17, means "pre-" or "prior to" primarily in terms of time and secondarily in terms of rank. According to all the Jewish wisdom authors (including John and Paul), God brought forth or created His personified firstborn Word/Wisdom *before* the physical universe was created. Then He created all things *through* His firstborn Word/Wisdom, which was later embodied in Yeshua's life and teachings. [cf. John 1.1-3; 1 Corinthians 8.6] So, in Colossians 1.17, when Paul pictures Yeshua metaphorically as the one who "is *before* (*pro* πρὸ) all things," we understand that "before" all things applies both in terms of time and of rank. Likewise, the author of Revelation 3.14 states that Yeshua is "the beginning or chief (*hay arxay* ἡ ἀρχὴ) *of* the creation of God (in both time and rank)."

5) "all things hold together in him"

Philo expands his portrayal of the first-created *Logos* (Word) as being God's (personified) firstborn son in terms of importance or rank. He portrays God "setting His true Word that is (His metaphorical) firstborn son over the heavenly bodies, who shall take upon himself the heavenly bodies' government like a viceroy of a great king." [*Agr.* 51] Further, Philo refers to "God's firstborn (son) as the Word who holds the eldership among the angels, their ruler as it were…" [*Confl.* 146] So, also, in Sirach 43.26, we read, "By (God's) Word all things hold together." And, the author of Hebrews 1.3 asserts that God bears or sustains (i.e., manages, maintains, and preserves) all things by His powerful Word, which is reflected by His son (Yeshua) whom He (the Father/Creator) appointed to be the heir of all things (in terms of rank).

In Colossians 1.16-17, Paul also portrays Yeshua metaphorically as the ranking firstborn *of* all creation, the one "in whom all things hold together." And, just as "the head of the body" is the most important part of the body, so also the "firstborn among many siblings" is the first ranking son among many siblings. [Colossians 1.18; Romans 8.29]

Conclusion

Genesis 1.3, "God said, 'Be light'…And it was so." Consequently, because Yeshua embodied the Word/Wisdom in his life and teachings, *Shaool* (Paul) portrays him metaphorically in Colossians 1.16 as the one "in/because of whom were created all things in the heavens and on the earth, the visible and the invisible…"

A Christian responds, "Your Jewish Wisdom literature, like the *Targumim*, the Midrash, the Mishnah and the like, I do not hold sacred or feel credible because it is compiled by men who didn't truly know their God as Yeshua himself spoke about this very subject of 'not knowing God.' 'O righteous Father, indeed □the [Jewish] world did NOT know You□, but I knew You, and these [12 men] knew that You sent Me.' (*Yohannan* 17:25) Thank you for your time and explanation, though."

It is misleading to insert "Jewish" in *YoHanan* (John) 17.12. It is more accurate to translate/interpret this verse as follows: "Righteous Father/Creator, the (non-*Torah* observant) world does not know you, but I know you; and these (i.e., my disciples who are faithfully obedient to Your Instruction/Word) know that You have sent me."

Note that Jewish Wisdom literature begins with Proverbs and continues through the centuries with additional Jewish works, including the book of John and parts of Paul's letters. The earlier Jewish Wisdom writings influenced *YoHanan* and *Shaool*. In other words, Yeshua's Jewish disciples, including *YoHanan* and *Shaool*, did not exist in a non-Jewish "Christian" vacuum uninformed by the Jewish world and its literature in which they lived and expressed themselves. Consequently, one should take *YoHanan*'s and *Shaool*'s Jewish learning, into account when interpreting their writings.

Section One: "In the Beginning Was the (Spoken) Word"

The Alleged "Eternal Son"

A Christian claims, "The Son is absolutely NOT a duplicate of the Father. In John 10:20, Jesus clearly says, 'I and the Father are One.' The clear context is that Father and Son are *Echad* (One). They have existed together from eternity past and will exist together for all eternity in the future."

If they (Father and son) "existed together from eternity past...," they could have a Father and son relationship. Two co-eternals would have a twin brother relationship, instead of a father-son relationship.

God, the Father/Creator, spoke or brought forth the personified firstborn, the first-created Word "*in*/at the beginning." We do not read "*before* the beginning" or in "eternity past." The Jewish authors of the Jewish Scriptures never claim that "the Word" existed "from eternity past." Later pagan Christians made up that false claim. If they both "existed together from eternity past...," how could one be the Father and the other be the son?

A Christian answers, "That is a very good and...difficult question. When we pray to the Father, both the Son and the Holy Spirit hears. When we pray to the Son, both the Father and the Holy Spirit hears. Sometimes the persons are easily distinguished by the context of the meeting.

"For example, twice the Father said, 'This is My beloved Son, in whom I am well pleased.' (Luke 3:32 and Matt. 17:5) Clearly, the Father spoke from the heavens while the Son was on the earth. So, we can distinguish between each other sometimes."

It is easy to tell who is "God, the Father" and who is the human son in the context of the original Jewish scriptures since they address each other as "Father" and "son." In the original Jewish context, no one claims that the human son is co-equal, co-eternal with the Father as later Christians do. Note that if the imaginary Christian son is co-eternal with the Father, no one would be able to tell which is the Father and which is the son.

A Christian responds, "I must disagree with your term 'imaginary Christian son.' One of the fundamental beliefs Christians hold is that the 'man' known as Jesus in the New Testament is exactly the same man referred to in Isaiah 53. Further, we believe the root of Jesse referred to in Isaiah 53:2 is the same root of Jesse referred to in Isaiah 11:10. If you agree that those two references are about the Messiah, then we are in agreement with who the Messiah truly is. Christians also believe that this Messiah, born of woman, is the same 'Lamb slain from the creation of the world.'"

The mortal human Yeshua *ben Yoseph* should be viewed as a metaphorical "son" of God who was born to human parents during the reign of King Herod. He is a metaphorical or spiritual "son" of God because of his faithful obedience to his Father/Creator. We, too, become metaphorical "sons" or "children" of God by faithful obedience to the Father/Creator. [John 1.12; 1 John 3.1,2; Rom. 8.14; Phil. 2.15]

However, the "imaginary (pagan) Christian son," is the one who allegedly existed along with the Father/Creator "from eternity past." Jews/Israelites never claim or hint anywhere

in the Jewish Scriptures that God's mortal human servant in Isaiah 53 existed "from eternity past."

A Christian responds, "I was disappointed to find that you didn't answer, nor even acknowledge my question about the 'root of Jesse.' Please tell me what you believe about the 'root of Jesse.' Do you believe they were the references to the coming Messiah? If not, what do you actually believe about the Messiah? Do you believe He is real? Has He already come? After several millennia, man has been saying He is coming, is He still coming? Like many Christians, I believe the Messiah is coming soon, but how soon I have no guess."

Yes, Isaiah 11.2 refers to the future Messiah as a descendant of *Yeeshai* (Jesse). When Isaiah says that the spirit of *HaShem* (י-ה-ו-ה) will rest upon "a shoot from *Yeeshai*'s stump," he does not mean that God's spirit would rest on a co-equal, co-eternal god-man. In contrast to the Christian "Jesus" who allegedly has no earthly father, the future Messiah would be a human patrilineal descendant of David and his father, *Yeeshai*.

If the alleged pagan Christian "Son" is a co-equal, co-eternal God person who existed "from eternity past," in what sense is this "Son" distinguished from his "Father/Creator"? Two co-equal, co-eternal Creators could not and would not have "a Father-Son" relationship.

A Christian responds and asks, "So, do you believe that in John 10:30 when Jesus said 'The Father and I are One' it shows that Jesus is speaking falsely?"

No, Yeshua is *not* speaking falsely. Nevertheless, many often misinterpret him. In John 10.30, when Yeshua says, "I and the Father are one, he means that because of his faithful

obedience to the Father that he is one *with* his Father/Creator. Yeshua does *not* mean that he is one and the same as his Father/Creator or that he is the Father/Creator.

Again, when Yeshua claims to be one *with* his Creator/Father (*HaShem*), he is indicating that he is one in full obedient agreement/cooperation with his Creator/Father. He is *not* saying that he is one and the same as his Creator/Father. Similarly, when a wife claims to be one *with* her husband, she is indicating that she is one in full agreement/cooperation *with* her husband. She is not claiming to be her husband.

It makes no sense for the human servant/son of God (Yeshua) to claim oneness with his Master/Creator (*HaShem*) if he is one and the same as the Master/Creator he obeys, worships and serves. However, it does make sense for the human servant/son of God (Yeshua) who obeys, worships and serves his Master/Creator to claim oneness with his Master/Creator (*HaShem*) on the basis that he is in full agreement/cooperation with Him and obedient to Him.

A Christian reasons, "Since [as far as I can tell] time began with the creation of the world. So, the term 'eternity past' is very hard to explain, let alone define. For convenience, I would call it "everything that happened before God began His creative acts…. God is eternal. He does not depend upon anything for His existence, even time. When God chose to create for six days, He created everything His creation needed to exist, including time. Since all of creation [including time] is finite, and God is infinite, God exists [present tense] before time and after time."

The adjective "before" refers to a time "before" another time. If there is a time before the beginning of time, then how could it be the beginning of time?

A Christian answers, "I submit: 1) God is eternal; 2) God is the Creator of all things, including time; 3) God chose to create everything in six days. If all of the above three statements are true then:

a) God existed before time, which is supported by all of the statements 1), 2) and 3).

b) The concept that time existed before God created all things is contradicted by statements 2) and 3).

If God requires time in order to exist, then time must be eternal, and therefore, at least equal to God. I do not believe anything has ever existed, which is even remotely equal to God. I believe you are having a problem with God's ability to exist without time, but that would make God subservient to time."

There is no problem with the Father/Creator's "ability to exist without time." Furthermore, it is true that nothing "has ever existed, which is even remotely equal to (the one and only) God (the Father/Creator)." As Yeshua said, "the Father is greater than I." [John 10.29; 14.28] But I reject the claim that any mortal human creature like Yeshua or even the personified firstborn Word existed "without time." As John clearly stated, *"In the beginning* was the Word." He did not say that the spoken first-created Word existed *"before* time," or *"outside of* time," or *"from eternity past."* Later, pagan Christians made that up.

A Christian claims, "Since the Son was there during all of the creation week (John 1:1-4), it is common sense to conclude the Son was there before the creation week began, just as was the Father (*Elohim*) Genesis 1:1 and was the Holy Spirit (*Ruach*

Elohim) Genesis 1:2. And the Son (*YHVH*) Genesis 1:3. Also, look at John 1:4-5, where Jesus was seen to be the light. Also, look at John 1:14, where we find that 'the Word became flesh and dwelt with us…'

"See all ten verses in Genesis 1 that include [God said…] these are the WORDs of God that created the world and are referred to in John 1:1."

The firstborn, first-created Word was next to its Creator "in/at the beginning (of creation week)" But, nowhere in the Jewish Scriptures are we told that the first-created Word was present "*before* the creation week."

The (Spoken) Word/Wisdom Was "in the Beginning" *Not* "in Eternity"

A Christian claims, "Yeshua is from eternity, and that is the beginning in which John speaks. The Word was God and created all things. All things that were created must include space and time. You are now contradicting yourself because before you stated that Yeshua is the first of creation, which would mean by your admission, He existed in eternity. Now you are saying He was created at birth. Which one is it? I think you do not believe that Yeshua is the only-begotten Son of God."

There is a significant difference between saying the Word/Wisdom is from "the beginning" and claiming that the Word/Wisdom is from "eternity" (which has no beginning). Saying that the spoken Word/Wisdom was with its Creator "in (the) beginning" (Ἐν ἀρχῇ *En arxay*) does

not mean it "existed in eternity." **The personified first-created "firstborn of creation,"** *HaShem*'s **Word/Wisdom, is the instrument or means** *through* **or** *by* **which the sole Source-of-All (***HaShem***) created everything, including space and time. While the personified Word/Wisdom is "the first of [the Creator's] creation (in the beginning)," this Word/Wisdom is not embodied in the historical Yeshua's life, works, and teachings until much later in history.**

A Christian responds, "The word 'beginning' in Greek is '*arche*' which means 'origin and literally the initial (starting) point.' Now when the passage does not indicate the Word being created in the beginning. God was also mentioned in the beginning, so whatever you say about 'the Word,' then you must apply to God. Genesis 1 states that in the beginning, God created the Heavens and the earth. So, if the Word is created, was He created before the Heavens or in the Heavens? If you say before the heavens, the passage indicates by default, only God existed. If you say in the heavens, then you would contradict John, who says that the Word created all things. Please allow the text to define your theology and do not read into the text your theology."

Referring to *HaShem*'s **personified spoken Word/Wisdom as "the first** *of* **[the Creator's] creation" or "the beginning" or "the initial (starting) point" of His creation is found in various places in the Jewish literature. From Jewish literature, we learn that Jews consider the personified Word/Wisdom (a.k.a. Instruction/***Torah***/Law), to be the firstborn** *of* **the created order. For example, in** <u>Genesis Rabbah</u> **i, 1, p. 2, we read, "With '***resheet***' (beginning) God created, and '***resheet***' means none other than** *Torah***, as it is said, '***HaShem*** made me,** *resheet***, as the beginning of His way." [See also** <u>Genesis Rabbah</u> **8:2] In another source, we find, "Seven things were created before the world was created:** *Torah***, repentance, the Garden of Eden,** *Gehinnom***,**

the Throne of Glory, the Temple, and the name of the Messiah. *Torah* -- 'HaShem acquired me [His *Torah*], the first of His ways, before His works of yore.' " (B. Talmud, *Pesachim* 54a) as quoted in *Mikraoth Temimoth - Mishlei* (Kesher Books).

So also, *Ben Sira* writes: "Wisdom was the first of all created things... It is [HaShem] Who created her...." [1.4-9] "I came out of the mouth of the Most High and covered the earth as a cloud/mist. Then the Creator of all things gave me a commandment, and the One, Who created me assigned a place for my tent. And He said, 'Make your dwelling in Jacob; find your heritage in Israel.' From time immemorial, in the beginning, He *created* me; and for the distant future, I shall not cease to exist." [24.3, 8-9] Furthermore, in the ancient book of Wisdom 9.9, we read: "Wisdom is with You (HaShem), who knows Your works and who was present when You made the world...."

The identification of the personified first-created "Wisdom" with the firstborn "*Torah*" or "Word" of God is ancient. This identification is evident, for example, in the <u>Book of Sirach</u>, when "Wisdom" declares: "Then the Creator of all things gave me a command, and my Creator chose the place for my tent. He said, 'Make your dwelling in Jacob and in Israel receive your inheritance.' Before the ages, in the beginning, He *created* me, and for all ages, I shall not cease to be. In the holy tent, I ministered before him, and so I was established in Zion. Thus, in the beloved city, he gave me a resting place, and in Jerusalem was my domain. I took root in an honored people, in the portion of the LORD, his heritage. ...Whoever obeys me will not be put to shame, and those who work with me will not sin." Then the Book of Sirach adds, "All this is the book of the covenant of the Most High God, the *Torah* that Moses commanded us as an inheritance for the congregations of

Jacob." [29.8-23; see also L. Ginzberg, *Perusheem veHiddusheem beeY'rushalmee*, IV, 1961, p. 20]

Since Yeshua embodies the personified firstborn Wisdom/Word in his life and teachings, it is not surprising to find that Jewish writers in the Renewed Covenant Scriptures identify him metaphorically as God's firstborn Word or Wisdom. In Revelation 3.14, for example, John figuratively refers to Yeshua, who embodies the (spoken) Word/Wisdom as "the beginning (chief) of God's creation." Furthermore, Paul identifies Yeshua allegorically as the firstborn Word or Wisdom when he teaches, "He (Yeshua) is an image of the invisible God, firstborn *of* all [God's] creation. [Col. 1.15-20] Likewise, in 1 John, we read, "...you have known him [the firstborn Word/Wisdom] who is from the beginning." [2.13] The "firstborn" of any group or family belongs to the group or family of which one is the firstborn. Since Yeshua is the "firstborn *of* creation," he belongs to the class of that which is created, including human creatures.

Another Christian asks, "Are you saying that there was a time when the Word was not?"

HaShem spoke, brought forth, or created the personified Word in the beginning [of time]. So how could there be "a time" when it "was not"?

The Firstborn Word/Wisdom Has *Not* "Always Existed"

A Christian argues, "Shmuel Playfair, your articles are awesome if you are trying to teach your theology. However, you still have not shown me in the scriptures or a Hebrew definition that would indicate that firstborn means first-created. Firstborn is a terminology that refers to prominence and preeminence and not being created."

Although the title "firstborn" does indicate "prominence and preeminence," it also assumes a beginning or birth for human creatures, including Yeshua. Therefore, the title of "firstborn" is never applied to the Greater Than All, the Father/Creator (*HaShem*) Who has no beginning and no birth. Since the title "firstborn" is synonymous with "first created," there is no reason to suppose that "firstborn" applies to the "unborn" or "uncreated" Father/Creator.

A Christian responds, "False assumption. There are two different words used in Greek for firstborn and first-created. I still have yet to see where Yeshua was created. Please show me a passage and not an interpretation."

There are two different words in both Greek and English for "firstborn" and "first-created." Nevertheless, they can be and should be understood as being synonymous in both English and Greek.

A Christian responds, "Shmuel Playfair, what rule are you using to state that "*protoktizo*" (first-created) and "*prototokos*" (firstborn) are synonymous? Please share or admit that you are wrong on this subject."

Common sense dictates that "Creator" is synonymous with "Father" even as "creature" is synonymous with "son." So, also "being created" is synonymous with "being born." The designation "the firstborn (*prototokos*) of creation" refers to one who is "*of* creation" and indicates/assumes a first-

created (*protoktizo*) beginning. **In other words, "*protoktizo*" (first-created) and "*prototokos*" (firstborn) are synonymous. So, "the first-created" Word/Wisdom is naturally "the firstborn" Word/Wisdom of God's creation. Note that the faithfully obedient human son of God, Yeshua, who embodied the (spoken) Word/Wisdom in his life and teachings, is a created creature like all other faithfully obedient human sons/children of God.**

A Christian answers, "It is the issue of cultural context. The Bible wasn't written in English. It was written in Hebrew, Aramaic, and Koine Greek. Therefore, we must explore what these words meant in the original languages and not read it from a 21st Century paradigm. If you do a word study on Firstborn in every passage of scripture, you will see that it deals with inheritance, prominence, and preeminence. It has nothing to do with creative order. For instance, Isaac is Abraham's firstborn, even though Ishmael is his first son. Another example is Jacob, who is firstborn over Esau. Firstborn in Jewish culture speaks more to the handling of the father's estate, and they are seen as being equal in authority to their fathers in business negotiations. Now Paul states that Yeshua is 'Firstborn of creation' and 'Firstborn among the dead.' Why? Colossians 1:18b states, 'that in everything He might be preeminent.' Simply put, He has dominion over all creation, including the dead. If Paul wanted to imply that Yeshua was first-created, then he would have used the Greek word *Protoktizo*, which actually means 'created first.' "

The personified "firstborn" Word/Wisdom in the Jewish Scriptures should be understood as both the "beginning" (ἀρχὴ *arxay* // רֵאשִׁית *resheeth*) *of* God's creation and as "the firstborn" (הַבְּכוֹר *hab'khor*) *of* God's creation. [cf. Rev. 3.14; Col. 1.15, 16] And, the metaphorical "firstborn son," Yeshua, who embodies the Word/Wisdom in his life and teachings, is also the Creator's primary heir (i.e., the one

who holds the rights and responsibilities of the firstborn son among many brothers.) [cf. Rom. 8.29; Heb. 1.2]

When Paul refers to the historical human Yeshua as "the firstborn *of* creation" in Colossians 1.18, he alludes to Yeshua's embodiment of the firstborn spoken Word/Wisdom in his life and teachings. In Colossians 1.18, the Greek designation "*prototokos*" (πρωτότοκος) and its Hebrew equivalent "*b'khor*" (בְּכֹר) both mean "firstborn" and *primarily* indicate "one who first opens the womb" or "one born first." Nevertheless, both the Greek and the Hebrew words also carry the connotation of one who is "first in rank." Thus, it is a mistake to claim that the designation "[firstborn] has nothing to do with creative order." While the Hebrew and Greek words meaning "firstborn" do carry a *secondary* implication for the laws of inheritance, these terms do not primarily relate to the laws of inheritance. For example, even though *Yaakov* (Jacob) purchased his older brother's birthright (בְּכֹרָה *b'khorah*) along with its blessings, *Esav* (rather than *Yaakov*) is still referred to as being *YeetzHak*'s (Isaac's) "firstborn" (בְּכֹר *b'khor*) regarding his order of birth. [Gen. 27.19, 32]

Only the one who is "*born of* creation" can be appointed as the heir to carry the birthright (בְּכֹרָה *b'khorah*) of the "firstborn" (הַבְּכֹור *hab'khor*) son. While Adam rather than his multi-great-great-great grandson, Yeshua, was historically born first, the much later "son of Man/Adam," Yeshua, became the rightful heir for the birthright (בְּכֹרָה *b'khorah*). Yeshua's Jewish followers considered their human master to be a created human being like Adam, who was created in his Creator's image or form/likeness. They never considered Yeshua to be the one and only Creator, the single Source *from* Whom are all things. [1 Cor. 8.6] https://www.facebook.com/notes/who-is-yeshua/the-firstborn-of-creation/235436886524294

A Christian responds, "Yes, there is still an implication of 'one being birthed,' which is the only way being 'firstborn' counts, but it does not automatically mean birth order in all applications. Going back to Jacob and Esau. Esau was Isaac's firstborn naturally. However, he was not his firstborn in regards to preeminence and inheritance of the promise given to Abraham and Isaac."

Esav remained Isaac's firstborn or first-created son, even when he sold the prerogatives or privileges of his birthright to his twin brother Jacob. The transfer of the prerogatives of birthright did not mean that Jacob suddenly or magically became Isaac's first-created or firstborn son in terms of birth order.

A Christian continues, "God refers to Israel as His firstborn son in Exodus 4:22. Israel was not the first created nation, nor was individual Israel the first to open the womb. The principle regarding the firstborn we see in Exodus 13:1."

The nation of Israel is considered to be *HaShem*'s metaphorical "firstborn son" because the people of Israel are the first and only nation He metaphorically procreated or brought forth to serve and worship him. [cf. Ex. 4.22]

A Christian adds, "As the firstborn is the Lord's possession, Yeshua fits this perfectly as He is the firstborn son of Mary. However, it is nowhere implied that Yeshua is created. He eternally existed as God in the person of the WORD."

The personified Word/Wisdom is portrayed as being next to its Creator "in the beginning" rather than as "eternally existing." Claiming that Yeshua, who later embodies the

Word/Wisdom in his life and teachings, is "not created" would mean that he is "not a human creature."

A Christian continues, "Again, the Word was with God, and the Word was God, and the Word became flesh. John 1:18 states that He was [in] union with Father and is the only [one] who has seen the Father and the only one who can reveal the Father."

Again, we are told in John 1.1 that the spoken Word was "*in* the *beginning*" *not* "in eternity." In other words, the fact that the personified Word/Wisdom who was the expression of the God/Power was born, brought forth, or first spoken "in the beginning" clearly indicates that this secondary, expression of "God" did not exist eternally. Only "*the* [Most High] God, the Father/Creator, from Whom the Word/Wisdom sprang or came forth, has "eternally existed."

A Christian argues, "In regard to Yeshua as the Son of God. We must understand what this means in the fullest context. Yeshua calls Himself 'the only-begotten' Son of God. 'Only-begotten' is the Greek word '*Monogenes*,' which means 'one of a kind' or 'unique.' This implies that He has a nature like the Father, which is why the Jewish leaders wanted to stone Him. Calling Himself the Son of God, or stating that 'God is His Father' implied equality with God in their mind. This was also why the apostles in some of their letters emphasized 'God the Father of our Lord Jesus Christ.' They understood that Yeshua is God in the flesh."

Calling Yeshua "the only begotten son" of God is an inaccurate and misleading translation of the Greek word "*monogenes*." Rather than "only-begotten" son, this word

should be translated as "one-of-a-kind" (i.e., unique) son. "*Monogenes*" (μονογενὴς) is the Greek equivalent of the Hebrew word "*yaHeed*" (יָחִיד only one). As we read, "...God tested Avraham and said to him, '...Please take your son, your only one (יְחִידְךָ *y'Heedkha* = your *monogenes* = unique), whom you love.' " [Genesis 22.2 cf. Jud. 11.34; Ps. 25.16] *Avraham* had at least two sons at the time, so *YitzHak* (Isaac) was not his only son. Instead, he was his "unique" son, who was especially loved.

Calling oneself "the (metaphorical) son of God" does not imply equality with God. Furthermore, referring to "God, the Father of our Master Yeshua, the Messiah," is not understood as meaning that "Yeshua is God in the flesh." These foreign ideas were made up by the later pagan church fathers.

https://www.facebook.com/notes/135740466493937/There%20Are%20Many%20%22Sons%22%20of%20God%20and%20One%20%22Specially%20Loved%22%20(Unique)%20%22Son%22/576080379126608/

A Christian continues, "Are [we] sons of God? Yes, because Paul stated in Romans 8, "For all who are being led by the Spirit of God, these are sons of God. 15 For you have not received a spirit of slavery leading to fear again, but you have received a SPIRIT OF ADOPTION AS SONS by which we cry out, 'Abba! Father!' We are adopted into sonship, not by nature. The scripture teaches that Yeshua is the Son of the Most High God because He was conceived by the Holy Spirit. 1 John 4:14 states, 'And we have seen and do testify that the Father sent the Son to be the Saviour of the world.' The Word became Flesh and appeared to us as Yeshua, the Son of the Living God."

God has many sons and daughters, but His unique son (His "*yaHeed*" יָחִיד) is Yeshua. Calling one of many children, your "unique son" who is "especially-loved," has *nothing* to do with being a "son by blood" as opposed to being a son by adoption. Also, being the faithfully obedient unique [metaphorical] son of God" does *not* imply that Yeshua has the Creator's far greater "nature" or "essence." When Yeshua calls God "my Father" or when he refers to the Creator as "our Father," that does not imply "equality with God," Who is far greater than humankind, including Yeshua. [cf. John 10.29; 24.28]

A Christian continues, "If the Word was God, then He is eternal and uncreated because *YHWH* is eternal and uncreated. Facts, not fiction."

While the firstborn spoken Word is the expression of its Creator and is sometimes called "God/Power" in the book of John, the first-created Word is not the Most High God, the Father/Creator Who spoke the Word in the beginning. The Word, which is called "God" (i.e., a secondary "Power"), is born, brought forth, or created by its Creator "in the beginning." This "God"/Power is *not the* Most High God (*HaShem*) Who the (spoken) Word was with or next to in the beginning. Only the Most High God, the Father/Creator (*HaShem*), "is eternal and uncreated."

A Christian responds, "In regard to 'the Word was with God and was God,' we should let John explain it: 'No one has ever seen God; The ONLY GOD, WHO IS at the Father's side, He has made Him known.' - John 1:18"

The variant Greek text for the English translation one quoted is false. It makes *no* sense to say that "no one has ever seen God" and then claim that "the ONLY GOD,"

which in context refers to Yeshua, whom many have seen "has made Him known." God, the Father/Creator, is the invisible, immortal "Spirit" Who has *never* been seen in the flesh as was Yeshua. [cf. John 1.18; 4.24]

A better translation for John 1.18, would say, "No human being has ever (physically) seen the [Most High] God [the single Creator/*HaShem*]. The unique (*monogenes*" μονογενὴς) son (i.e., Yeshua who is visible and mortal), the one who is in the bosom/lap (i.e., who lives in harmony with the will) of his Father/Creator, that one made Him (his Creator) known (ἐξηγήσατο *exagaysato*)." In other words, Yeshua reported, interpreted, explained, or revealed the Father's character/will.

A Christian continues, "Yeshua has always existed. His physical body was the only thing that was not in existence. Hebrews 10:5 states, 'Consequently, when Christ came into the world, he said, 'Sacrifices and offerings you have not desired, but a body you have prepared for me.' Yeshua is the Eternal God by nature, but His physical body had a beginning date. Interestingly enough, His physical [body] doesn't have an ending because He is physically seated on the throne in Heaven on the right hand of the Father, reigning in a place of power and honor as having all authority and sharing the glory as *YHWH*."

Neither Yeshua nor the firstborn Word/Wisdom has "always existed." Instead, the personified Word/Wisdom embodied in the life and teachings of the historical human Yeshua is first spoken, "in the beginning." The single Source of all that is, *HaShem*, Who has no beginning or birth, brings the Word/Wisdom forth as the means or instrument by/through which He creates all things. The personified firstborn, first-created Word/Wisdom embodied in the life and teachings of Yeshua, can and should be embodied in all of Yeshua's disciples.

In Psalm 40.7-9/6-8, King David acknowledges that the Creator has prepared a body for him in which to do His will because doing his Father's will is what *HaShem* desires rather than "sacrifices and offerings." The author of Hebrews 10.5 applies this passage to David's patrilineal offspring, Yeshua. So, the claim that Yeshua, a mortal son of David, "is the [immortal] Eternal God by nature," is not supported by anything we read in Hebrews.

Yeshua's physical body had a decisive ending when he was crucified on a Roman cross. Yeshua is given *temporary* authority as *HaShem*'s human representative. [cf. 1 Cor. 15.23-28] Also, the single Creator does not share His glory with any of His creatures, including Yeshua, the Son of Man/Adam. [cf. Isa. 42.8, 11]

"In (the) Beginning Was (ἦν *Hain*) the (Spoken) Word (λόγος *Logos*)"

In John 1.1-3, the personified Word/Wisdom *through* which the Father/Creator created the world is portrayed as being with/next to the single Father/Creator "in (the) beginning" rather than eternally. Also, the Jewish wisdom writers always portrayed the personified "Wisdom" or "Word" *through* which the Creator created all things as being birthed, made, brought forth, or created at/in the beginning of creation. Consequently, the (spoken) Word/Wisdom is characterized in the Jewish Scriptures as being "the firstborn *of* (God's) creation" in contrast to the single Creator *from* Whom alone are all things. [cf. 1 Cor. 8.6]

A Christian responds, "John did not say his being with the Father, IN THE BEGINNING, was THE beginning for THE existence of this word, for he used the imperfect tense *ην*."

The context given for the Greek verb "ἦν" (*"hain"* translated as "was") in John 1.1a is *"in/at* the beginning" [*not "before* the beginning" *and* not "in eternity"].

A Christian responds, "In the beginning …So, what does that mean? When time started! If I say, 'John was living when it all started,' does it not imply that John had been living BEFORE it all started? The problem is you are deliberately ignoring the use of the imperfect tense *ην*, which ought to be literally translated as 'was existing.' So, an accurate interpretive translation will be given thus: 'When time started the word was existing, and the word was in the same class with God.' I repeat, John was only showing how the word predates time, as it were."

Also, another Christian asks, "Are you saying that there was a time when the Word was not?"

Nothing, not even the metaphorical firstborn Word/Wisdom is "in the same class with God, the eternal/unborn Father/Creator." *HaShem* created or gave birth to His personified Word/Wisdom *in/at the beginning* [of the *time* of the process of creation]. So how could there be "a *time*" when "the Word was not?

We are informed in Jewish wisdom literature that the Creator's Word/Wisdom was "acquired," "given birth," or "created" *in/at* the beginning of His (the Father/Creator's) way. The firstborn Word/Wisdom was the foremost (beginning) of His acts of yore, and therefore was existing

(ἦν *hain*) *at/in* the beginning of the creation process. [cf. Prov. 8.22-31; Rev. 3.14, et cetera] The illustrative analogy that because "John was living when it all started" implies "that John had been living BEFORE it all started," is not applicable to that which "was existing (ἦν *hain*) in/at the beginning (of the time of creation)." Speculation regarding existence at a *time* "BEFORE (the) time all (of creation) started" or a *time* that "predates time" makes no sense. However, it *does* make sense to say that the firstborn Word/Wisdom was acquired or created first and therefore was existing (ἦν *hain*) "in/at the beginning" of the entire creation process.

A Christian continues, "John 1:1 c used ην, a be - verb, not as a substantive verb (i.e., a be - verb expressing existence, as in John 1: 1 a & b), but, as a copulative verb expressing equation. In other words, by virtue of the Greek emphatic word order, John 1: 1 c actually ought to read either as 'and the word belonged to the class of God', or as 'and the word was categorized as God.' Now, what this means is that the Word possessed God's attributes and the New English Bible is close to bringing what John had in mind (when he threw θεος, a predicate nominative, to the front for emphasis) to the fore by translating it as, 'and what God was, the Word was.'" Now, let me point out that the issue is not whether the Word was the same in identity with God the Father - for John already showed the difference in identity when he wrote,' and the word was existing NEAR God.' -but the issue is that the Word possessed God's exact attributes."

Yes, in John 1.1c, the Word *was* copulative/equivalent to or representative of *the* God/Power (the Father/Creator) and therefore called "God/Power." So, it would be better to translate this as "and what God was, the Word was." So, this secondary, representative "God/Power" was *not the* Most High God/Power (the Creator) Whom the personified Word was with/next to in the beginning. In other words, this Word was the expression of God and was *not "the* God" (the single Father/Creator) Who spoke, acquired, created, or birthed the Word/Wisdom "in the beginning."

While the personified Word (called "God") *represents* and *reveals* the single Creator Who spoke, acquired, or created it, nowhere are we told that the firstborn Word "possesses" the single Creator's "exact attributes." For example, Jews *never* characterized the Word as being the only Source *from* Whom are all things (including the personified firstborn Word/Wisdom). [cf. 1 Cor. 8.6] Also, the first-created Word is never portrayed as having no beginning or as being "the only one having immortality" or as being "the God no one has ever seen nor can see." [cf. John 1.18; 1 Tim. 6.15-16]

Later, Yeshua, who embodies the (spoken) Word in his life and teachings, consistently refers to the Most High God Whom he worships and serves as being the invisible "Spirit" Who was *greater* than himself. [cf. John 4.24; 10.29; 14.28] Neither Yeshua nor any other Jewish author ever characterize the single Creator as being a human creature whom many see in the flesh. In contrast to the Most High God Who was never given anything by anyone else, Yeshua, who embodies the firstborn, first-created Word in his life and teachings, receives temporary authority and power, which he will surrender back to his Father/Creator in the end. [cf. 1 Cor. 15.24-28]

No Time "Before" the Beginning of Time

A Christian states, "You say that God created the Word of God = Wisdom of God. So now, according to your theory, God had no wisdom before HE created HIS Wisdom."

The personified firstborn/first created Word/Wisdom by which the Creator created all things was next to its Creator "in the beginning." There is no time "before" the beginning when the Father created the heavens and the earth. While the single Source of all that exists has no beginning and is never "born" nor "of creation," the Creator's personified Word/Wisdom is the "firstborn *of* all creation." [cf. Col. 1.15]

A Christian responds, "Shmuel Playfair, sir, I love your patience and astute way of commenting."

HaShem Created Me (the Firstborn Word/Wisdom) in the Beginning

The creation begins "in (the) beginning" (בְּרֵאשִׁית *b'resheet* = Ἐν ἀρχῇ) when "God created the heavens and the earth." [cf. Gen. 1.1] The personified firstborn Word/Wisdom, which is the first-created accomplishment *of* the created order, is the subservient, subsistent (dependently existing) *means* or *agent by* or *through* whom the Father/Creator created all things. Paul makes a clear distinction between the Creator and His firstborn, first-created Word/Wisdom when he writes, "Yet for us, there is one God, the Father, *from* Whom are all things...and one Master, Yeshua the

Messiah (who embodied the Word/Wisdom in his life and teachings), *through* whom are all things...." [1 Cor. 8.6]

A Christian asks, "Where does it say the Word was created?"

The following four notes found in Jewish wisdom literature discuss Wisdom's creation, Wisdom's presence with its Creator in the beginning, and Wisdom's identification as the Word or the Instruction/*Torah*/Law of God:

1) As to Wisdom's creation, in Proverbs 8.22-36, we find: "*HaShem* (י-ה-ו-ה) brought me (Wisdom) forth, created or acquired me (*kananee* קָנָנִי, which is a poetic use of the verb *kanah* קָנָה meaning "acquired") at the beginning of His way, before His deeds from of old. From time immemorial, I was appointed from the beginning of the world. When there were no oceans, I was given birth when there were no springs abounding with water. Before the mountains were settled [in place], before the hills, I was born... Then I was a craftsman [*amon* אָמוֹן = marksman] beside (next to) Him (the single Creator). And I was delighting day by day rejoicing before Him (in *HaShem*'s presence) all of the time."

2) Also, regarding Wisdom's creation, Joshua *ben Sira*, a Jewish wisdom author, explains in the book of Sirach (a.k.a. Ecclesiasticus): "Wisdom was the first of all created things... It is [*HaShem*] Who created her...." [1.4-9] And later, we read, "I (Wisdom) came out of the mouth of the Most High and covered the earth as a cloud/mist. Then the Creator of all things gave me (Wisdom) a commandment and the One Who created me assigned a place for my tent. And He said, 'Make your dwelling in Jacob; find your heritage in Israel.' From time immemorial, in the beginning, He *created* me; and for the distant future, I shall not cease to exist." [24.3, 8-9]

3) Concerning the personified Wisdom being with or next to its Creator in the beginning, we read in the book of Wisdom 9.9: "Wisdom is with You (*HaShem*), who knows Your (*HaShem*'s) works and who was present when You (*HaShem*) made the world...."

4) Regarding the ancient identification of personified "Wisdom" with the "*Torah*" or "Word" of God, in the Book of Sirach (Ecclesiasticus) by Joshua *ben Sira*, "Wisdom" declares: "Then the Creator of all things gave me (Wisdom) a command, and my *Creator* chose the place for my tent. He (*HaShem*) said, 'Make your dwelling in Jacob and in Israel receive your inheritance.' Before the ages, in the beginning, He *created* me, and for all the ages, I shall not cease to be. In the holy tent, I ministered before him, and so I was established in Zion. Thus, in the beloved city, He gave me a resting place, and in Jerusalem was my domain. I took root in an honored people, in the portion of the LORD, his heritage. ...Whoever obeys me will not be put to shame, and those who work with me will not sin." Then ben Sira adds, "All this (regarding Wisdom) is the book of the covenant of the Most High God, the *Torah* that Moses commanded us as an inheritance for the congregations of Jacob." [29.8-23; see also L. Ginzberg, *Perusheem veHiddusheem beeY'rushalmee*, IV, 1961, p. 20]

Paul teaches, "He (Yeshua, who embodies the Word/Wisdom in his life and teachings) is an image/form or design of the invisible God (just as Adam, the first-created man is an image/form or design of God). He (i.e., the (spoken) Word embodied in Yeshua's life and teachings) is the firstborn *of* all [God's] creation. [Col. 1.15-20] Note that when Paul identifies Yeshua as the embodiment of the firstborn Word/Wisdom, he does not mean that the historical Yeshua existed as a visible person at the beginning of creation.

HaShem "created," "gave birth to," or "brought forth" the "firstborn *of* creation" (the personified Word/Wisdom) when He spoke, "in the beginning." [cf. Gen. 1.1-26] Remember that all the Jewish writers clearly distinguish the firstborn, first-created Word/Wisdom from the single Source of all creation, the Father/Creator, Who brought forth/created His firstborn, first-created Word/Wisdom in the beginning.

Hokmah (Wisdom), and *Logos* (Word), and *Torah* (Instruction)

Being "set up," "given birth," "formed," or "acquired" are different ways of referring to *HaShem*'s creative work. Here is the translation of Proverbs 8.22-25 given in the ArtScroll *Tanach* Series: 22 *HaShem* made (i.e., acquired) me at the beginning of His way, before His deeds of yore. 23 I reigned since the distant past: from the beginning, from before [there was] the earth. 24 When there were no depths, I was formed; then there were no springs abundant with water, 25 before the mountains were settled, before the hills, I was formed (literally "given birth"). So, *HaShem* (the sole Creator) created, set up, gave birth, formed, or acquired Wisdom (a.k.a. the firstborn Word or the Instruction/*Torah*/Law) before He created the world (*Rashi*).

Literally, *kananee* (קָנָנִי) means "acquired me." The Creator acquires something by creating it. See, for example, Genesis

14.19 where we read, בָּרוּךְ אַבְרָם לְאֵל עֶלְיוֹן קֹנֵה שָׁמַיִם וָאָרֶץ: **Blessed is Avram of God, the Most High, Possessor (or Maker) of heaven and earth." Whatever the Most High makes or creates, He possesses.**

Someone remarks, "*Elohim* is the causative in all his creation. He never had to acquire anything. *Hokmah* (Wisdom) exists because He does; there is nothing outside of Him. Prov 22 is nothing more than poetic prose, giving *Hokmah* a voice and personifying it into a woman."

As noted above, *Elohim* "acquires" something by creating it. How would one translate Proverbs 8.22?

Someone answers, "OK. First of all, I think that there is too much emphasis being placed on words here. This is part of Jewish Wisdom literature, and like Job is poetic prose where imagery is the main focus. I could just as easily say, for verse 22, 'YHWH revealed me in the beginning of his way.' Since *Hokmah* (Wisdom) is really what is being shown here in the creation process, these verses (in Proverbs eight), which are foundational for Jewish Wisdom literature, use poetic imagery. But my primary focus here is trying to understand the meaning of the poetic truth(s) being expressed."

The inadequate English translation "*HaShem* revealed me (personified Wisdom) ..." leads to a misleading interpretation of Proverbs 8.22. The Hebrew verb, "*kananee* (קָנָנִי)," means "acquired, possessed, created, formed, or established me/Wisdom" rather than "revealed me/Wisdom."

Note that the root word for "*kananee*" is *kanah* (קָנָה), which signifies "to get, gain, purchase, obtain, acquire, form, make, erect (i.e., create)." Due to the different connotations or uses for the Hebrew root (קָנָה) *kanah*, this root verb is

translated into English in various ways. For example, (קָנָה) *kanah* is used in the sense of "to found" or "to form [the heavens]" (cf. Gen. 14.19,22), "to beget [a son]" (Deut. 32.6), "to acquire" [a man, strategies, wisdom, or understanding] (cf. Gen. 4.1; Prov. 1.5; 4.5, 7), "to purchase [a field]" (Gen. 25.10), and "to possess or own [a heart of understanding" or "to be an owner"] (Prov. 15.32; 19.8; Isa. 1.3). [cf. Gesenius, Davis, and Strong]

Also, note that in Proverbs 8.22-31, the verb, "*kananee* (קָנָנִי)," meaning "acquired me" or "created me" is parallel in meaning both to "set up" or "established me" (נְסַכְתִּי *neesakhtee*) and "brought forth" or "birthed me" (חוֹלָלְתִּי *Holaltee*).

The Septuagint translates the Hebrew verb, "*kananee* (קָנָנִי)," as "ἔκτισέν με (*ektisen may*)" meaning "created, fashioned, made me/wisdom." Furthermore, the *Peshitta TaNaKh* also paraphrases this word as meaning "created me/wisdom." Also, later Jewish Wisdom authors such as Ben Sira use the Greek verb, *ktizo* (κτίζω), meaning "created" when speaking of Wisdom's origin (cf. Ecclus. 1.4, 9-10; 24.3, 8-9).

In the Talmud, we read that seven things which were created by *HaShem* preceded the creation of the world: *Torah*/Wisdom, repentance, the Garden of Eden, Gehinnom, the Throne of Glory, the Holy Temple and the name of the Messiah. [*PesaHeem* 54a] And according to the Midrash (*B'resheth Rabbah* 1:5), the *Torah* and the Throne of Glory were created before the world. At the same time, other things such as the name of the Messiah were considered to be existing only in the Creator's thought/planning. While "Your Throne was established from times of yore" (Ps. 93.2), the Wisdom of the *Torah* was created "before His deeds of yore" (Prov. 8.22).

Consequently, we can safely assume that much more than "revealed [me]" is meant regarding personified Wisdom's origin in Proverbs 8.22. Instead of personified Wisdom simply being "revealed," it is rather "acquired, possessed, created, formed, or established" as/at the "beginning of [*HaShem*'s] way, before His deeds of yore."

Someone continues, "Wisdom comes before the 'spoken word.' They are not the same. They are two different processes with two different words. Even the Holy One has to have a plan, a design before it can be spoken into existence: 'I was set up (revealed) at the first, before the beginning of the earth.' (Pro 8:23). It's all imagery being shown here.

"*Elohim* did NOT create Wisdom as if it wasn't already within him. He is Wisdom. People quote John 1 as the *logos*, which was a concept of an external source. There are a few translations that have correctly used Wisdom instead of logos. 'In the beginning, was Wisdom and Wisdom was with *Elohim*, and Wisdom was *Elohim*.'

"'Wisdom was created before all things, and prudent understanding from eternity. The root of wisdom-- to whom has it been revealed? Her clever devices -- who knows them? 6 There is One who is wise, greatly to be feared, sitting upon his throne. 7 The Lord himself created wisdom; he saw her and apportioned her; He poured her out upon all his works.' (Sir 1:4-7) Once again, imagery."

The Creator's personified "Wisdom" (חָכְמָה *Hokhmah*) in Hebrew, and His personified "Word" (λόγος *Logos*) in Greek are two different words with different meanings in two different languages. However, the close similarity between them should not be overlooked, minimized, or

denied. Philo teaches that "Wisdom" could be considered to be the metaphorical mother of both the Word (*Logos*) and the cosmos. [Fug. 108-9] And he defines "Wisdom" as "the land of the Word (*Logos*)." [Migr. 28] Also, Philo identifies the *Logos* as being God's "firstborn son." As we read, "...He appoints as their immediate superintendent, His own right Word (*Logos*), His firstborn son, who is the lieutenant of the great King..." [On Husbandry XII 45]

Note that the Jewish Wisdom writers characterize both Wisdom and Word as "the firstborn" of God's creation and the "beginning of His way." Furthermore, both function as the agent or means by/through which the Most High created the world. It is no wonder that Philo and later John both use the Greek term "*Logos*" for the role and function of personified Word/Wisdom.

The identification of "Wisdom" with the Instruction/*Torah*/Law" or "the Word" of God is ancient. For example, in the Book of Sirach, "Wisdom" declares: "Then the Creator of all things gave me a command, and my Creator chose/fixed the place for my tent. He said, 'Make your dwelling/tent in Jacob and make Israel your inheritance.' Before the ages, in the beginning, He created me, and for all the ages, I shall remain/not cease to be. In the holy tent, I ministered before him, and so I was established in Zion. Thus, in the beloved city, he gave me a resting place, and in Jerusalem is my domain (i.e., where I wield my authority). I took root in an honored (privileged) people, in the portion of the LORD, in His heritage (inheritance). ...Whoever obeys me will not be put to shame, and those who work with me will not sin." Then Sirach adds, "All this is the Book of the covenant of the Most High God, the *Torah* that Moses commanded us as an inheritance for the congregations of Jacob." [29.8-23; see also L.

Ginzberg, "*Perusheem veHiddusheem beeY'rushalmee*," IV, 1961, p. 20]

The single Creator is indeed "wise, greatly to be feared, and sitting upon His throne." However, Jewish Wisdom writers portray the personified expression of the Creator's Wisdom/Word through which He created all things as being "created," "made," or "birthed" in the beginning. As we read, "He (*HaShem*) saw her (personified Wisdom) and apportioned her and poured her out upon all His (*HaShem*'s) works [of creation]." [Sir. 1.4-7]

In other words, the personified firstborn of creation (a.k.a. God's Word/Wisdom) is not considered to be another co-eternal being or a second creator, but rather the subservient instrument/means or agent through which *HaShem* created all things. Throughout the scriptures, Jewish authors distinguish between *HaShem*, the single Source of all that is, and the personified Word/Wisdom, the instrument/means or agent through which the Father/Creator created all things. [cf. Prov. 8.22-25; John 1.1-3; Col. 1.15-20]

Note that the Jewish antecedent for something being called the "firstborn" (πρωτότοκος *prototokos* = "the one born first" = בְּכֹר *b'khor*) of God's creation is found with regard to God's personified "Wisdom." [cf. Prov. 8.22-25; Philo, De Ebrietate 30-31, Quaestions in Genesis 4.97; De Virtutibus 62] "Firstborn" in the context of Proverbs 8.22-25 refers not only to one who is considered to be the first-created accomplishment, but also as one who takes precedence over the rest of creation. As soon as one uses the term "firstborn" or "of creation" it should be obvious from a Jewish point of view that this does not refer to the "unborn," invisible Creator, the single Source of all creation including His subsistent (dependently existing), subservient Word/Wisdom.

Someone continues, "Paul never once referred to Yeshua as *Logos* but as the *Hokmah* of *Elohim* revealed. A plan that was hidden until the right time."

Throughout Jewish scripture and wisdom literature, writers depict God's Word, Wisdom, or *Torah*/Instruction as being "the image of God," which was created or brought forth as "the firstborn of creation." [Prov. 8.22-25; Fug. 108-9; <u>On Husbandry</u> XII 45; <u>Conf. Ling.</u> 146; see also <u>Agric.</u> 51; <u>Som.</u> 1.215; et cetera] In Colossians 1.15-20, Paul continues in this Jewish tradition. He refers to Yeshua (who embodies Gods' Word/Wisdom or *Torah* in his life and teachings) as being both the "image of the invisible God" (εἰκὼν τοῦ θεοῦ τοῦ ἀοράτου) and as the "firstborn of all creation" (πρωτότοκος πάσης κτίσεως).

Note that Paul, like John, depicts Yeshua as one who embodies God's Word/Wisdom and Instruction/Law in his life and teachings. In other words, they picture Yeshua as the human representative of the Creator's Wisdom/*Hokmah*, Word/*Logos*, or Instruction/*Torah*. So, they portray Yeshua metaphorically as both "the firstborn of all creation" and as "the beginning of God's creation." [cf. Col. 1.15; Rev. 3.14]

The Firstborn Word *"through/by* Which Are All Things"

All things are created *through* or *by* the spoken Word/Wisdom of the single Eternal Creator. In other words, the personified Word/Wisdom "*through* whom are all things" is distinct from the Eternal Creator "*from Whom are all things.*" [cf. 1 Cor. 8.6]

A Christian responds, "If Yeshua was created, then all things were not created through Yeshua."

When an author says that all his literary works of art are created *by* or *through* his words, we understand that the author first creates or gives birth to his words as he puts those words into writing. The first-created, firstborn words become the instrument/means or the agent *by* or *through* which the author forms all his literary works. In the final analysis, *all* the author's works of art are composed by the author's first-created, firstborn words.

When John says that "all things" were created *by/through* God's personified spoken Word, we should understand that God first created or gave birth to His Word. The first-created, firstborn Word became the instrument/means or agent by or through which God created all things. Note that God's firstborn, first-created Word later became embodied in Yeshua's life and teachings. In other words, the historical human Yeshua did not exist at the time God created all things.

A Christian responds, "ALL THINGS is ALL THINGS. The Gospel of John declares that without Yeshua, nothing came into being that was made. This is a contradiction if Yeshua was created because he came into being according to you. Look at the Genesis account. God created the Heavens and the earth. Where in the *Torah* does it state that God created a creator? Where would John get this additional insight?"

"ALL THINGS" means all things which were created by means of or through God's firstborn, first-created personified Word.

No one is saying that "God created a [second] creator." Instead, the sole Source of all that is (*HaShem*, the Father/Creator) brought forth or first formed His personified Word/Wisdom by or through which He created ALL THINGS.

https://www.facebook.com/notes/the-firstborn-word-wisdom/he-hashem-created-me-the-firstborn-word-wisdom-in-the-beginning/213307922029546

A Christian responds, "Where are you getting the notion that firstborn means first-created? Again, if all the scriptures are in sync, then the only creator is *YHWH*. John testifies that the WORD was with God and was God. John does not make a distinction between the Word being God and God, who created all things. So how do you make that distinction? Again, firstborn does not mean first-created."

Many people mistakenly suppose that "firstborn" equates to "unborn" or "uncreated" Father/Creator. On the contrary, "firstborn *of creation*" refers to one who is "born" and also implies one who is "first-created" by the Father/Creator. Yes, *HaShem* is "the only Creator." So, John makes a crucial distinction between "the Word was [called] 'God'/Power" and "*the* [Most High] God/Power" Whom the firstborn, first-created Word is with or next to or in the beginning.

https://www.facebook.com/notes/the-firstborn-word-wisdom/firstborn-of-creation/352637838096553 https://www.facebook.com/notes/the-firstborn-word-wisdom/this-god-was-next-to-the-god-in-the-beginning/214366848590320

A Christian continues, "Firstborn does not mean first-created! Where does that show up in the Hebrew language? If birth was given to Yeshua, where in the *Tanakh* states this? If you say, Proverbs 8:22, then make sure you look at Proverbs 8:1 to get the full context which clearly does not speak of Yeshua."

"Firstborn" is synonymous with "first-created" even as "the Creator" is equivalent to "the Father" and as "son" is synonymous with "creature." Paul refers to Yeshua as being "the firstborn among many siblings." [Rom. 8.29; Col. 1.15] In other words, he holds leadership for all who belong to the category of those who are created, born, or given birth. However, all who are created or born should be distinguished from the single Father/Creator Who is never created or born. That which is created or born includes the personified first-created, firstborn Word/Wisdom and later the historical Yeshua, who embodies the (spoken) Word/Wisdom in his life and teachings.

https://www.facebook.com/notes/135740466493937/A%20%22Begotten%22%20Son%20is%20a%20%22Created%22%20Son/884417071626269/

The Firstborn *of* Creation

Many Christians rely on a *mis*translation of Colossians 1.15, which reads, "He (Yeshua) is the image of the invisible *Eloheem* (God), the firstborn *over* all creation."

Nevertheless, the verse reads, "...the firstborn *of* (*not over*) *all creation.*" In the first part of Colossians 1.15, we find that there is a crucial difference between being the historical human Yeshua who is created like Adam in the *image* of the invisible *Eloheem*, the Father/Creator (*HaShem*), and being the invisible God, the Father/Creator, *HaShem* Himself.

In the second part of Colossians 1.15, the expression "firstborn *of creation*" refers to the firstborn, first-created Word/Wisdom, which later becomes embodied in the life and teachings of Yeshua. Thus, the expression "firstborn *of creation*" assumes that both the personified Word/Wisdom and later the historical Yeshua belong to the created order. Also, Colossians 1.15 carries the idea that a "firstborn son" is a place or position that implies one is a son/creature, not a father/creator. On the other hand, the single Creator, Who is far greater than Yeshua and Who is *never* "born *of* creation," would therefore *never* be referred to as "the firstborn *of* creation" or as "the firstborn among many brothers." [cf. Romans 8.29]

A Christian responds, "David was called 'the Firstborn,' yet he was the youngest of Jesse's ten sons! It was a position of honor and majesty that one was placed in..... 'I will place him as Firstborn, higher than all the kings of the earth.' (Ps 97:7-NWT)"

King David is *never* considered to be "the firstborn" son of Jesse. Instead, in Psalm 97.7, David is regarded as the "firstborn, higher than all the kings of the earth." Generally speaking, besides referring to birth order, the designation "the firstborn" also indicates "a position of honor and majesty" in which one is placed. However, notice that the designated "firstborn" Yeshua, like his ancestor King David, is one of the human kings or human creatures among whom he is considered to be the "firstborn, higher than all the kings of the earth." [cf. Psalm 97.7]

"Firstborn" indicates not only a position of authority but also to "a birth" or a beginning, as the word itself indicates. One cannot be in a position of *first* born or *first* created if one does not belong to the category of those who are *born* or *created*.

A Christian responds, "What category was David, the FIRSTBORN, inasmuch as he obviously was 'created' last amongst Jesse`s ten sons?"

Yeshua, like his ancestor King David, belongs to the category of creatures, sons, or brothers among whom they were born. Moreover, first David and later Yeshua, are depicted as the firstborn of the kings of the earth. [Ps. 89.27; Rev. 1.5; cf. Rom. 8.29]

A Christian responds, "But this BEGS the question...if He was 'created' last, how and why then is he called 'the firstborn'???"

While the "firstborn" is "a position of honor and majesty" in which King David and later Yeshua is placed, Adam (not David or Yeshua) is actually created first. Yet, the Greater-Than-All, the single Creator, exalted Yeshua, a son of Man/Adam and a descendent of David to the position of being the "firstborn" of all His creatures, higher than all the human kings of the earth by making this human creature to be "the firstborn from the dead." [cf. Colossians 1.18]

When Yeshua is identified as "the faithful and true witness, the beginning (first or chief) *of* the creation of God" in Rev. 3.14, that does not mean he is present as a visible historical person because humankind has not yet created. Instead, what is present at the beginning of creation is the personified firstborn, first-created Word/Wisdom, which is later embodied in the historical Yeshua's life and teachings. On the other hand, the one and only Creator, the Father *from* Whom are all things and the One Who is far greater than any of His creatures (including Yeshua) is *never* considered to be either "*of* creation" or "firstborn."

Paul clearly distinguishes between the one and only Father/Creator and the firstborn Word/Wisdom later embodied in the life and teachings of Yeshua. Both the personified Word/Wisdom and the later historical Yeshua are of the created order: "Yet for us, there is one God, the Father (i.e., the Creator = the *Ayn Sof* (אין סוף) = *HaShem*) *from* Whom are all things...and one Master, Yeshua (who embodies the firstborn, first-created personified Word/Wisdom in his life and teachings), the Messiah *through* whom are all things...." [1 Cor. 8.6]

A Christian responds, "Why didn't Paul use the Koine Greek word that literally DOES mean "first-created, to wit, *Prototkistos*, instead of *Prototokos* (firstborn)? Wouldn't that have settled the matter?"

Why did Paul use "Father" rather than "Creator" in 1 Corinthians 8.6? All who are "born *of* creation" are considered to be literally "*of creation*." [cf. Colossians 1.15] "Firstborn" (*prototokos*) is a close synonym to "first-created" (*prototkistos*) in the same way that "the Father" is a close synonym for "the Creator." In other words, referring to the personified Word/Wisdom as "the firstborn *of* creation" is a picturesque, poetic way of saying "the first-created *of* creation."

While the Creator "had no beginning," He spoke or brought forth His Word/Wisdom "in the beginning." Furthermore, the personified firstborn, first-created Word/Wisdom became flesh (i.e., was embodied in the life and teachings of the historical person named Yeshua *ben Yoseph*) later in history. [cf. John 1.14] While the Creator's Word/Wisdom "came forth" from the Eternal God, *in* the *beginning*, only the Father/Creator Himself had *no* start and was *never* born or created.

A Christian responds, "But the WORD, being ALSO the SON, could not have been a created being, and therefore of more recent origin than the Father, for it is impossible to think of the Father as ever being without that Eternal WORD."

Since the Father/Creator has *no* origin or beginning or end, it makes no sense to speak of a "more recent origin than the Father" Who has *no* origin. However, the Eternal Father/Creator, Who alone has *no* "source" or beginning or end, should be distinguished from His firstborn, first-created Word/Wisdom, which He created, setup, gave birth to, or brought forth *in the beginning*. Also, it makes no sense to speak of a "time before the beginning" when referring to one born or created "in the beginning." The personified firstborn Word/Wisdom that was brought forth by its Creator, in the beginning, is portrayed throughout Jewish wisdom literature as being the first accomplishment or expression of God's creation.

The (Personified) Firstborn Word/Wisdom Portrayed as the Metaphorical "Firstborn Son"

A Christian writes, "Paul wrote [in] Colossians 1:15, 'He is the image of the invisible God, the firstborn of all creation; 16 for in him all things were created, in heaven and on earth, visible and invisible, whether thrones or dominions or principalities or authorities--all things were created through him and for him. 17 He is before all things, and in him, all things hold together. 18 He is the head of the body, the church; he is the beginning, the firstborn from the dead, that in everything he might be preeminent. 19 For in him all the fullness of God was pleased to dwell, 20 and through him to reconcile to himself all things, whether on earth or in heaven, making peace by the blood of his cross.'"

Paul wrote that the same "fullness of God" found in the firstborn child *of* creation is also pleased to dwell in all the other children of God. [cf. Eph. 3.19]

A Christian responds, "But you're ignoring the rest of it. Jesus is the divine Creator. He is, in essence, the same Word through which God created the universe."

Paul does *not* imply that "Jesus is the divine Creator." Instead, he views Yeshua as the embodiment of the firstborn, first-created personified Word/Wisdom. The (spoken) Word/Wisdom is the subservient agent *through* whom the Father/Creator creates the universe. Neither the firstborn Word/Wisdom nor the later historical Yeshua is "the divine Creator" Himself.

A Christian responds, "Nobody is questioning that God used His word to say, 'Let there be light.' What we're talking about is Paul's claim that Jesus is the one through whom the world was created. The universe was actually created *for* Jesus. And even more significantly, it was created *through* Jesus. This means that he was God's instrument of creation. The one doing the creating and the one for whom it was created were one and the same Being!"

The one Father and His personified firstborn Word/Wisdom or the single Creator and His first-created Word/Wisdom agent should always be regarded as being two different identities and *never* viewed as one single identity or as "one and the same Being."

A Christian responds, "John chapter one identifies the Word of God as being both God and with God... John 1:1, 'In the beginning was the Word, and the Word was with God, and the Word was God.'"

John identifies the spoken Word as "God/Power," which is next to *the* Most High "God" (the ultimate Source of Power), in the beginning. He draws inspiration from the Jewish Wisdom literature, which depicts the (spoken) Word as a dependent, secondary "God" or "Power." The authors of Jewish Wisdom literature had no idea that later pagan Christian idolaters would misinterpret their words. These idolaters twisted the Jewish imagery of the firstborn Word/Wisdom into a proof text for claiming that Yeshua, a mortal human creature, is co-equal, co-eternal with the immortal Creator.

A Christian answers, "Nevertheless, this 'Word' that was next to God is identified in John one as God Himself!"

Not true! In John 1.1-3, the personified Word, who is secondarily given the title of "God" or "Power," is portrayed as being *next to* "the God" Who spoke it, brought it forth, or created it in the beginning. The secondary "God/Power" is never identified as being the Most High God Himself. Also, it makes no sense for God, the Creator, to be "next to" Himself.

A Christian responds, "And that's why it's not described in just that way, though the implication is there. God is in eternity with His word 'by His side.' The word of God was at His disposal in the same way that your mouth is at your disposal. And since God's word became God's firstborn, a man, it can be said that God's infinite Being can stand side by side with any verbalized expression of Himself He wishes to create, just as His word was at His disposal from the beginning."

The personified Word/Wisdom is pictured or portrayed in Jewish wisdom literature as being the Creator's "firstborn *of creation*" **before it becomes embodied in the life and teachings of Yeshua, a historical human creature. In other words, the single Creator Who has** *no* **equal spoke the Word/Wisdom into existence in the beginning. In John 1.1-3, the personified Word/Wisdom, which is called "God/Power," was** *beside* **(or next to)** *the* **Most High God Who created, made, or brought it forth in the beginning.**

A Christian responds, "There is a discussion of God's wisdom being the 'first of God's works' in creation. Where does God call His word or wisdom 'His firstborn'? My understanding of 'firstborn' relates to a firstborn child, a human being. Jesus is God's firstborn child because he was the first man to have been born, who is also God.

"The word of God began to speak prior to creation. It did not mean God's word as an entity had a beginning. It was just when God began to speak in terms of creation. The word of God was not previously a 'firstborn Son.' Rather, the human Son of God had been the word of God prior to his incarnation."

Note that in Jewish Wisdom literature, the personified *Logos* **(Word) is the Greek equivalent of the Hebraic** *Hokhmah* **(Wisdom). The literature in both languages**

refers to the Word and Wisdom as "the firstborn of God's creation." The designation of "the firstborn" implies the idea of "the firstborn son." For example, in Prov. 8.22, we find Wisdom saying, "*HaShem made* (*acquired*) *me at the beginning of His way, the first of His works of old.*" Philo writes, "...God's firstborn [son], the Word, who holds the eldership among the messengers, their ruler as it were...." [Conf. Ling. 146; see also Agric. 51; Som. 1.215] Philo also calls the *Logos* "the eldest of all *created* things." [Leg. All. III.175; cf. Ebr. 132f.]

A Christian responds, "I understand what the Jews meant. I don't, however, understand what you mean. You apply 'the firstborn son' to Jesus, whereas the Jews do not. They simply poetically apply the designation 'Son' to God's word, which was the instrument God used in designing creation. But applying that 'word' to a human son is entirely different from the way the Jews meant to apply it. It required I believe, a Christian revelation to apply the word of God to Jesus."

Many years before the book of John and Paul's letters were written, Philo, a Jewish wisdom writer, identified Moses, "a human son," as "the law-giving Word." [cf. Migr. 23f; cf. 122] Philo also identified Moses as "...a living *Torah*/Law (νόμος ἔμψυχος *nomos empsychos*)." [2 On the Life of Moses I, 4] So also, *YoHanan* (John) portrays the personified "firstborn" (metaphorical son), *HaShem's* Word present at creation, as being embodied in the life and teachings of the historical Yeshua. [cf. John 1.14]

Note that when the Jewish author of Revelation 3.14, characterizes the human Yeshua as "the beginning (or chief) *of* the creation of God," he understands that the historical Yeshua was not literally or physically present at creation. Instead, the (spoken) Word later embodied in the life and teachings of Yeshua was present at creation. Like the author of Revelation 3.14, Paul likewise identifies Yeshua metaphorically as being the "firstborn *of* all creation." [Col. 1.15-17]

A Christian responds, "I do agree with you that God's word assumed the form of human flesh. That is, Jesus came to speak and act in a perfect correlation with God's word. This doesn't make God's 'word' a 'firstborn son.' Rather, it means that God's word assumed the form of His 'firstborn son' when it took the form of Jesus."

Being born or created first "in the beginning" before the rest of creation implies that the personified "Word" is also considered to be the Father's firstborn, first-created metaphorical "son." Therefore, in John 1.14, it makes sense that the personified Word, the Creator's "firstborn son," is portrayed as becoming embodied in the life and teachings of the human Yeshua.

==

Paul also refers to Yeshua as the Word/Wisdom, which is the "firstborn *of* all creation." [Col. 1.15-17]

A Christian responds, "No, he doesn't. He references the term 'firstborn' to God's Son. Col. 1: He has delivered us from the dominion of darkness and transferred us to the kingdom of His beloved Son... He is the image of the invisible God, the first-born of all creation... Technically, the Word of God *became* the Son. The Son had existed formerly as 'the eternal word of God.'"

In Jewish wisdom literature, the personified Word is referred to as "the firstborn *of HaShem*'s creation," which is metaphorically understood to be God's firstborn *son*. According to John 1.14, long after creation, the firstborn

Word is expressed in the historical life and teachings of the Creator's faithfully obedient, human son, Yeshua.

A Christian responds, "Words mean what they mean *in context*. This means that although you can establish an identification between the Word of God, the Son of God, and Jesus, the man, this does not mean that these words or phrases are interchangeable. They each have their own specific meaning and context. You can say that Jesus had existed previously as God's 'word.' But you cannot say that the word of God prior to Jesus *was* Jesus or *was* the 'firstborn,' or *was* the Son of God. The word of God assumed the form of Jesus the firstborn Son in time. The 'word' did not have these qualities prior to the incarnation."

It is correct to say that the historical human creature, Yeshua, did *not* physically exist at the time of creation, *nor* did he exist as a mortal human person before he was conceived and born. However, according to Jewish Wisdom literature, the personified spoken Word/Wisdom, "the firstborn [metaphorical son]" *of* all God's creation, did exist since it was first born or first-created and therefore was present at the time of creation. Furthermore, just as Philo previously identifies Moses as "the law-giving Word," so also John later identifies Yeshua as being the firstborn Word. [cf. Migr. 23f; cf. 122; John 1.14]

Sometimes the Aramaic Expression *"Memra"* (מֵימְרָא) Meaning "the Word" Is Used as a Circumlocution for the Creator's Name

A Christian writes, "There are at least three main arguments about the source of John's *Logos* title, but I think that John Ronning in his book, <u>The Jewish Targums and John's *Logos* Theology</u>, makes a strong case that John got his title from the Targums. He points out that the targumists' main concern was the most appropriate way to speak of God in the synagogue setting. They rephrased many expressions which might suggest that there was something human about God. [pg. 17] »» The Targumic 'Word' is frequently employed in passages that speak of God's interaction with his creation, including humankind (especially His people), a fact consistent with the view that such usage is meant to guard the transcendence of God. In such passages, what the MT (Masoretic Text) ascribes to God, the Targums often ascribe to his Word. The Word is everything that God is supposed to be, and its manifold activity encompasses the entire spectrum of divine endeavor… As for the divine Word encompassing 'the entire spectrum of divine endeavor', we see in John's Gospel that the Son's activities encompass the entire spectrum of divine activity in the OT. John says that creation was accomplished explicitly through the Son (1:3), but in addition, John shows us that the redemption of Israel from Egypt was accomplished through the Son, who came down from heaven, the law was given through the Son, Israel was led through the wilderness by the Son, as his bride, and Israel had life by believing in the Son. The Targums employ Word in describing the works of God in all these categories… In many contexts, one could view the divine Word as a projection of the transcendent God into his creation. ««« [pg. 18]

"Ronning then shows in text after text that John describes activities of Yeshua that in the MT is ascribed to *HaShem* but in the Targums as the Word, the Word of the Lord or the Name of the Word of the Lord. Activities like:
• Creation

• Receiving/Not Receiving the Divine Word, believing in His Name
• the Word, Glory, and Shekinah
• the Word speaks to Nathanael about ascending and descending on the Son of Man

". . . John believed that this Word came down and became flesh and dwelt among us. This is the Word that in the *Targums* of the *Tanach* is clearly none other than *YHVH*. This is the Yeshua that John believed in. And I don't believe for a moment that John believed Yeshua was just a mere man and a great prophet. Now you might not agree that John made this link [between the Word (Yeshua) and *YHVH*], or you might think that John should have treated Yeshua as a mere man, but that doesn't negate the fact that John did [make a link between the Word (Yeshua) and *YHVH*]."

Jews have used different designations or expressions like "the Name" (*HaShem* הַשֵּׁם), "Heaven" (*Shamayeem* שָׁמַיִם), "the Power" (*Hag'vurah* הַגְּבוּרָה), and "my MASTER/LORD" (*Adonai* אֲדֹנָי) as circumlocutions (i.e., roundabout expressions) for the name of the Creator. So, also, the Aramaic expression, "*Memra*" (מֵימְרָא), meaning "the Word" was *sometimes* used in the *Targum*, the Aramaic translation or paraphrase of the Hebrew Scriptures, as a circumlocution for the Hebrew name of God. However, the Greek version of the Aramaic expression, "*Memra*" (מֵימְרָא), which is "the *Logos*" (ὁ λόγος), was *not* used as a circumlocution for the name of God in the book of John, the book of Revelation, or anywhere else in the Renewed Covenant Scriptures.

Note that John aligns with the Jewish wisdom tradition when he portrays the personified Word/Wisdom as the firstborn agent *by* and *through* which the single Creator, *HaShem*, created the world. And just as Philo refers to

Abraham as "the model of Wisdom" and Moses as "the law-giving Word," John portrays Yeshua as "the Word (Wisdom) become flesh [i.e., the Instruction/*Torah*/Law embodied in the life and teachings of Yeshua]." [cf. <u>On Dreams</u> 1. 69-70; <u>Migr.</u> 23.; cf. 122, John 1.14] But neither Philo nor John consider the three historical human beings, Abraham, Moses, and Yeshua, to be *HaShem*, the single Creator/Source of all creation. The single Creator alone is the Source of all things, including His firstborn subsistent, subservient Word/Wisdom, called "God/Power" *by* or *through* which all things are made. [cf. John 1.1-3]

https://www.facebook.com/notes/who-is-yeshua/moses-as-the-law-giving-word/240202876047695

https://www.facebook.com/photo.php?fbid=1112798475427053&set=a.158333104206933.29890.100000907332477&type=3&theater

Binitarianism?

A Christian claims, "All of those specific passages in Isaiah and whatnot, that were interpreted by Paul and others as speaking of Binitarianism (two powers in heaven) were called a heresy by OTHER Pharisees. Acts 24:14 'But this I confess unto thee, that after the way which THEY CALL HERESY, so I worship the God of my fathers, believing all things which are written in the law and the prophets.' "

Paul and the other Jews who wrote the Renewed Covenant Scriptures believed in one single God, the Father/Creator. These Jews did not believe in two co-equal, co-eternal powers (gods) or Binitarianism as found in Persian

Zoroastrian thinking or a trinity of God persons like later Christians claim. As Paul put it, "Yet for us, there is one (single) God, the Father, *from* Whom are all things...and one [human] Master/Lord, Yeshua the Messiah, *through* whom are all things...." [1 Cor. 8.6]   Also, in 1 Tim. 2.5, Paul wrote, "For there is one God; there is also one mediator between God and humankind, the man Messiah Yeshua." Paul, along with the other Jewish writers, clearly distinguish the one God, the Father/Creator, from the one Master/Lord, the human mediator between God and the rest of humanity.

A Christian responds, "No, now you are definitely mistaken. Binitarianism WAS NOT a Christian invention. It was Jewish all along. For centuries before the appearance of Jesus. This is the subject matter of the research by Seagal and Boyarin and other Orthodox Jews. Both Christian and Gnostics ran with it, but it was primarily a Jewish belief. Check your history facts."

The rabbis who spoke against two authorities, powers, or domains (רְשׁוּיוֹת *reshu'yot*) being in heaven were referring to the two co-equal gods found in Persian Zoroastrian theology or other theological discourse. The reference to two different powers/gods in Jewish wisdom literature is entirely different. When these writers spoke regarding a second power/god, they distinguished the one (single) Supreme Power, the ultimate Source of all that is, from the secondary, subservient power, the firstborn agent of the only Creator. They do not believe in two or three different co-equal, co-eternal powers as Zoroastrians, and later Christians imagine. Paul explicitly claims that "there is *one* God, the Father/Creator, *from* Whom are all things...." Christians and Binitarians will not be able to refute that! [For a critique of Boyarin's books take a look at the following:

A Christian responds, "No one is adding the co-equal part to this thread. That is being added by you. I am sticking to the Orthodox Jewish sources. Binitarianism is strictly Jewish. The belief was that there was an invisible *YHWH* King overall and a co-creator who was visible and called the *Memra* in the Targums. The Word a.k.a. *Dabar-YHWH* (Gen 15:2), who was visible and expected to incarnate as a man-God is an agent of the invisible but is still the same *YHWH*. So, it was never thought of as two gods. The two co-equal gods were how Gnosticism rationalized it. Two gods of which one was a lesser god and called the demiurge. But that is not Jewish binitarianism."

Christians (rather than myself) added the "co-equal, co-eternal" claim to the original idea expressed in Jewish wisdom literature to support their belief in a Threesome god. The visible human *agent* of the invisible *HaShem* is not "still the same *YHWH*." The firstborn "agent" of the Supreme Power, the single Creator (*HaShem*), is a different created or begotten "power" (not the same "Power") by definition.

A Christian responds, "No, the visible *YHWH* is the same invisible *YHWH*, but not quite. Ask any Jew familiar with the Targums, and he will tell you that the *Memra* is NOT another god but is visible."

The Aramaic expression, "*Memra*" (מֵימְרָא), primarily refers to "the (spoken) Word" of *HaShem*, not to the single Source of all creation, the Creator Himself. Moreover, Jewish wisdom authors portray the personified spoken "Word" as being *HaShem*'s subservient instrument or agent by whom or through whom the ultimate Sovereign created all things.

Also, the Aramaic Targums sometimes employ the expression *"Memra"* (meaning "the Word") as a circumlocution for the Creator's Hebrew name. However, Jews using this circumlocution understood the difference between these two different usages of the Aramaic expression, *"Memra."*

===

The Jewish belief regarding "two (unequal) powers (gods)" is mentioned most clearly in the Renewed Covenant Scriptures in the prologue to the gospel of *YoHanan* (John). Like Philo, who wrote a generation earlier, *YoHanan* distinguishes between *"ho Theos"* (ὁ θεὸς) meaning *"the God/Power"* Who has no beginning and Who "no man has ever seen" [1.18] and *"Theos"* (θεὸς) meaning "God/Power" whom "the God" brought forth *in the beginning.* [cf. Fug. 97; Sacr. AC.9; Som. 1:229-30; Leg. All., II, 86]

Before *YoHannan* wrote his gospel, Philo taught that "Nothing mortal can be made in the likeness of the Most High, the Father/Creator of the universe, but only in that of the secondary "God" who is His *Logos*." [Qu. Gen. II, 62] Further he explains, "...to whom God says, 'I am the God who was seen by you in place of God.' ['...ἐν τόπῳ θεοῦ *en topo theou*'; Gen. 31.13 LXX] ...but examine it accurately, and see whether there are really two Gods. For it is said: 'I am the God who was seen by you' not in My place, but in place of God as if he meant some other God. What then should we say? There is one true God only, but those who are called 'Gods' are numerous. On which account the holy scripture on the present occasion indicates that it is the true God that is meant by the use of the article, the expression being, 'I am the God (ὁ θεὸς *ho Theos*).' However, when the word is used [alternately], it is put without the article the expression being, 'He who was seen by you in the place,' not 'of the God (*tou Theou*)", but simply 'of God (θεοῦ *Theou*).' And what He calls 'God' is His chief Word...." [On Dreams, Book 1. 227-230]

Jewish wisdom writers applied the title "*Theos*" (God/Power) not only to THE Almighty (*HaShem* of Armies, the All-Powerful One Whom no man has seen or can see) but also to His firstborn creature, the personified Word. So, it is not surprising that both Philo and later John made use of the definite article "the" to distinguish the God (τὸν θεόν *tone Theon*"), the single Creator, from His Word who was called "God" (θεὸς *Theos*) on a secondary level. This secondary "*Theos*" (God) was next to (πρὸς pros = next to = secondary to) "*TONE Theon*" (THE God) in the beginning.

The firstborn of creation (i.e., the personified spoken Word) is considered to be the subservient agent or metaphorical architect through whom the ultimate Sovereign created all things. This first of *HaShem*'s creation is given God's name or authority, but he is not considered to be a second co-equal, co-eternal God-person. *HaShem* "created," "gave birth to," or "brought forth" the "firstborn of creation" (a.k.a. God's Wisdom, Word or Instruction) when He spoke, "in the beginning."

Jews portray the personified spoken Word as the auxiliary and subservient firstborn, first-created instrument or agent of creation, but *never* as the one and only single Creator, the From Whom are all things. So, we may recognize the historical human Yeshua (*not* the famous mythological virgin-born "god-man" Jesus) as a patrilineal son of David who embodied God's Word, Wisdom, or *Torah*, in his life and teachings. In other words, we may picture him as the *through whom* are all things (but *not* as the *From Whom* are all things).

Section Two: "And the (Spoken) Word Was Beside/Next To *the* [Most High] God…"

"…and the Word was beside/next to the (Most High) God (haEloheem) and the Word was God/Power (El). This one (called God/Power) was in the beginning with the (Most High) God. All things were made through it (the Word), and without it, not even one thing was made." [John 1.1-3]

The Personified Firstborn Word Was With/Next To Its Creator

A Christian writes, " 'In the beginning was the Word…and the Word was God…all things were made by him.' Pretty simple, eh?"

This quotation/translation from *YoHanan* (John) 1.1-3 skips a crucial distinction that would help keep *YoHanan*'s message in a proper perspective. *YoHanan* wrote, "In (the) beginning was the (spoken) Word, and the Word was with/next to *the* God (the single Creator), and the Word was 'God/Power.' This one [called "God/Power"] was associated with *the* God [Who first spoke/created it] in the beginning. Through/by means of it (the (spoken) Word), all things became…" Note that Jews like Philo taught the same thing regarding the Word (*Logos*) of *HaShem* many years before *Yeshua* was born, and the book of *YoHanan* was written. So, in John 1.1-3, we read that the Word called "God/Power" was with/next to *THE* (Most High) God/THE (Ultimate) Power Who spoke it, brought it forth or created it in the beginning.

Also, the book of Proverbs and subsequent Jewish Wisdom tradition portrays the firstborn of creation as the instrument/means, blueprint, or agent *by means of/through* which *HaShem*, the only Creator, creates the heavens and the earth. In order to correctly interpret *YoHanan* 1.1-3, one needs to read and understand the rich Jewish Wisdom literary tradition and thought from which *YoHanan* draws his inspiration.

The (Spoken) Word Called "God/Power" Was Next To/Beside or Assistant to *the* [Most High] GOD (πρὸς τὸν θεόν *Pros Ton Theon*)

We learn from the Jewish Scriptures and Jewish wisdom literature that God created the universe through His Word/Wisdom. The personified Word/Wisdom is the first act of creation and is called "the firstborn of creation." Note that the personified Word/Wisdom, the instrument/means or agent of creation, is beside/next to and assistant to the God, its Creator. Later, in John 1.14, the (spoken) Word is portrayed as becoming embodied in the life, works, and teachings of the historical Yeshua. In other words, whereas the spoken Word/Wisdom is present at the beginning of creation, the historical Yeshua does not yet exist.

John 1.18 goes on to teach, "No man has ever seen the GOD. The unique son (Yeshua), the one being in the bosom of the Father (i.e., the one doing *HaShem*'s will), declared Him (GOD)." Although no human being has ever seen the one and only Father/Creator, the historical human Yeshua reveals his God through the first-created Word/Wisdom, which he embodied in his life, works, and teachings. Note that the visible Yeshua is *not* the unseen God, but he reveals the first-created Word/Wisdom of the unseen Father/Creator in his life and teachings.

In <u>Genesis Rabbah</u> [i, 1, p. 2 See also 8:2], we read, "With 'רֵאשִׁית *resheet*' (beginning) God created, and "*resheet*" (רֵאשִׁית) means none other than *Torah*, as it is said, "*HaShem* (י-ה-ו-ה) made me "*resheet*" (at the beginning) of His way." Also, in the Talmud, we read, "Seven things were created before the world was created: *Torah*, repentance, the Garden of Eden, *Gehinnom*, the Throne of Glory, the Temple, and the name of the Messiah. *Torah* -- 'The LORD (*HaShem*) acquired (i.e., created) me [His *Torah*], the first of His ways, before His works of yore.' " (B. *Talmud*, <u>Pesachim</u> 54a) as quoted in *Mikraoth Temimoth* - <u>Mishlei</u> (Kesher Books).

Most Christians mistakenly assume that John 1.1 indicates that the Word is *not* created, because "the Word was with God and the Word was God." However, this faulty and misleading translation of John 1.1 fails to indicate the difference between the (spoken) Word who is called "God/Power" ("*Theos*" θεὸς) and "THE God/THE Power" ("*ton Theon*" τὸν θεόν) Whom the Word is next to or associated with, in the beginning. Consequently, most Christians misunderstand the subservient relationship between the subsistent (dependently existing) "God/Power" and *the* ultimate Most High God/Power Who created or brought forth His dependent and subservient Word in the beginning.

When interpreting John 1.1, keep in mind that in Jewish Scriptures and wisdom literature, the personified spoken Word/Wisdom (a.k.a. *HaShem*'s Instruction/*Torah*/Law) is considered to be the first accomplishment *of* the created order. Furthermore, this firstborn, first-created Word/Wisdom, which is beside/next to its Father/Creator, in the beginning, serves as the auxiliary, subservient instrument, means, or subordinate agent *by/through* which the Father/Creator creates all things. The Jewish authors of the wisdom literature also reveal that the personified first-created, firstborn Word/Wisdom is *given* the title "God/Power" in a secondary sense indicating it bears the Most High God's authority. Therefore, one should *not* consider the (spoken) Word to be a second co-equal, co-eternal God-person as later idolaters claim. In summary, *HaShem* created, gave birth to, or brought forth the "firstborn of creation" (a.k.a. God's Word/Wisdom or Instruction/*Torah*/Law) when He first spoke, "in the beginning."

A generation before the book of John was written, Philo taught, "Nothing mortal can be made in the likeness of the Most High, the Father of the universe, but only in that of a *second* "God" (i.e., "God/Power" in a secondary sense) who is His *Logos*/Word." [Qu. Gen. II, 62] And further he explains: "...to whom God says, 'I am the God, Who was seen by you in place of God (*en topo theou*).' [Gen. 31.13 LXX] ...but examine it accurately, and see whether there are really two Gods. For it is said: 'I am the God who was seen by you' not in My place, but 'in place of God' as if he meant some other God. What then should we say? There is one true God/Power only, but they who are called 'gods/powers' are numerous. On this account, the holy scripture on the present occasion indicates that it is the true God that is meant by the use of the article, the expression being, 'I am *the* God (*ho Theos*).' However, when the word is used [alternately], it is put without the article with the expression being, 'He who was seen by you in place,' *not* of '*the* God (*tou Theou*),' but only 'of God (*Theou*).' And what

He calls 'God' (without the article) is His chief Word...."
[On Dreams, Book 1. 227-230]

Like Philo, John (*YoHanan*) also distinguishes "*ton Theon*" (τὸν θεόν) meaning "THE God" Who has no beginning, and Whom "no man has ever seen" (John 1.18) from the firstborn Word called "*Theos*" (θεὸς) meaning "God/Power" whom "THE God" brought forth *in the beginning*. [cf. Fug. 97; Sacr. AC.9; Som. 1:229-30; Leg. All., II, 86]

The title "God/Power" (*Theos*) applies not only to THE Almighty, the All-Powerful Creator Whom no man has seen or can see but also to the Creator's firstborn, first-created Word/Wisdom. Consequently, Jewish wisdom writers used the definite article "THE" to distinguish THE God ("*ton Theon*" τὸν θεόν) from the first-created, firstborn Word. The personified Word was also called or referred to as "God" ("*Theos*" θεὸς) in a secondary, dependent sense. *YoHanan*, a Jewish wisdom author, pictures the secondary, subsistent (dependently existing), and subservient "*Theos*" (God/Power) as being beside/next to and assistant to (πρὸς *pros* = next to/associated with) "*TON Theon*" (THE God/the Ultimate Power).

===

A Christian asks, "Would it be wrong for God to claim to be God?"

There is an essential difference between the single Father/Creator (i.e., *the* one and only Most High God) and the firstborn, first-created Word/Wisdom embodied in the life and teachings of the historical Yeshua. It is *not* wrong to claim that the one and only Father/Creator is *THE* ultimate God/Power (τὸν θεόν *ton Theon*). However, it is a mistake to declare that Yeshua, who embodies the (spoken) Word/Wisdom in his life, works, and teachings, is the single Creator Who is Greater Than All.

A Christian then asks, "How do you explain the first verses of John, which say (I'm sure you know of it) that 'the Word was God,' and then a little later says that the Word became flesh?"

In the Jewish scriptures, titles like "King," "Master/Lord," and "God" have different levels or contexts of meaning. For example, Jews use the title "King" to refer not only to the various "kings of Judah and Israel," but also to the anticipated human "King Messiah" and to the single Creator, *HaShem,* as "the King of the Universe." Also, everyone can acknowledge that the title of "Master/Lord" might refer not only to "the Master/Lord of the estate," but also to the human messianic Master/Lord and to the ultimate Sovereign MASTER/LORD of the universe, *HaShem.* Similarly, we find in the Hebrew Scriptures that the title of "God" (*Eloheem*), meaning "Sovereign Power," is given not only to messengers (angels), *Moshe,* the judges, and the kings of Israel but also to the single Creator, *HaShem.* So, it is not surprising that Philo (a generation earlier) refers to the firstborn Word/Wisdom as "God" (in a secondary, subservient sense). Later, *YoHanan* (John) echoes Philo, saying that in the beginning, the personified Word who was called "God/Power" secondarily was beside/next to/associated with THE Most High God/Power, the single Creator.

A Christian responds and asks, "I don't understand. Are you saying that Scripture can say that someone or something is God from the beginning and not mean what it says? Or are you saying that the 'Word' used in verse 1 is used in a different context than the 'Word' in verse 14?"

Of course, Scripture means what it says. However, translators can and do mistranslate it, and their interpreters and readers can and do misinterpret it. We should understand the contrast between anointed human "Masters," "Kings," and "Gods/Powers" and the single Father/Creator, the ultimate "Master," "King," and "God," *HaShem*. In other words, we must discern or recognize the crucial difference between the personified "firstborn of creation," the (spoken) Word, which is secondarily called "God/Power," and "*THE* God/Power," the Ultimate Source of all, Who has no beginning and was never born. John portrays the personified spoken "Word," in John 1.1., as becoming embodied in the life, works, and teachings of the historical human Yeshua in John 1.14 and throughout the rest of the book.

==

The popular Christian phrase, "God the Son," is *not* found in John 1.1-14 nor anywhere else in the Renewed Covenant Scriptures. Also, the historical human being, Yeshua, was not present when the world was created. He had not yet been born or named. *YoHanan* (John) in John 1.1 follows the Jewish Wisdom tradition when he tells us that the world was created through/by means of God's personified Word/Wisdom or Instruction/*Torah*/Law. The (spoken) Word/Wisdom later became embodied in God's faithfully obedient son, Yeshua, who is now called the "firstborn" among many (faithfully obedient) siblings. [cf. John 1.14; Romans 8.29]

A Christian objects and says, "In John 17:5 Jesus explicitly states that he was with the Father before the world was created."

In John 17.5, Yeshua prays, "And, now, Father, glorify me with the splendor/glory next to Yourself that I was (destined) to have from You before the world existed." Yeshua's prayer does not mean that this historical mortal human being was literally, visibly present with God before He created the world. Instead, he requests the glory from his Creator that he was destined to receive before the world existed.

Note that Jews consider the personified Word (a.k.a. *HaShem*'s *Torah* that was beside/next to its Creator, the Greater than all, *in* the beginning) to be the firstborn of the created order. In <u>Genesis Rabbah</u> i, 1, p. 2, we read, "With '*resheet*' (רֵאשִׁית beginning) God created, and '*resheet*' means none other than *Torah* (Instruction), as it is said, '*HaShem* made me, *resheet*, as the beginning of His way.'" [See also Genesis *Rabbah* 8:2] Furthermore, we read, "Seven things were created before the world was created: *Torah*, repentance, the Garden of Eden, *Gehinnom*, the Throne of Glory, the Temple, and the name of the Messiah. *Torah* -- '*HaShem* acquired me [the personified Word or *Torah*], the first of His ways, before His works of yore.' " (B. *Talmud*, <u>Pesachim</u> 54a, as quoted in *Mikraoth Temimoth* - <u>Mishlei</u> Kesher Books). Also, as we read in Proverbs 8.22-31, "*HaShem* made (acquired = created) me at the beginning of His way, the first of His works of old... I was there when He set the heavens in place... Then I was a master craftsman [אָמוֹן *amon* = artisan] beside/next to Him (אֶצְלוֹ *etzlo*); and I was daily His delight, one always rejoicing in His presence...."

A Christian objects, saying, "The Word was not created. John writes, 'He was with God and was God.' " [cf. John 1.1-3] And another Christian asks, "Are you saying that the Word is not God?"

Like Philo, the Alexandrian Jew who wrote a generation earlier, YoHanan distinguishes between "*ho Theos*" (the God) Who has no beginning and Who "no man has ever seen" (1.18) from "Theos" (God) whom "the God" brought forth or created in the beginning. [cf. <u>Fug</u>. 97; <u>Sacr</u>. <u>AC</u>. 9; <u>Som</u>. 1:229-30; <u>Leg</u>. <u>All</u>., II, 86] Philo teaches before *YoHannan* was written, "Nothing mortal can be made in the likeness of the Most High, the Father/Creator of the universe, but only in that of the secondary "God/Power" who is His *Logos*." [<u>Qu</u>. <u>Gen</u>. II, 62] And further, he explains, "...to whom God says, 'I am the God who was seen by you in place of God (*en topo theou*). [Gen. 31.13 LXX] ...but examine it accurately, and see whether there are really two Gods. For it is said: 'I am the God who was seen by you' not in My place, but in place of God as if he meant some other God. What then should we say? There is only one true God; but they who are called 'Gods' are numerous; on which account the holy scripture on the present occasion indicates that it is the true God that is meant by the use of the article, the expression being, 'I am *the* God (*ho Theos)*'; but when the word is used [alternately], it is put without the article the expression being, 'He who was seen by you in the place,' *not* 'of *the* God (τοῦ θεοῦ *tou Theou*)," but simply '*of* God (θεοῦ *Theou*).' And what He calls 'God' is His chief Word...." [<u>On Dreams</u>, <u>Book 1</u>. 227-230]

Keep in mind that the word "*Theos*" (θεὸς God/Power) applies not only to THE Almighty, *HaShem* Whom no man has seen or can see but also to the firstborn *of* creation, the personified Word. Consequently, Jewish writers use of the definite article "THE" to distinguish "THE God (τὸν θεόν "*tone Theon*")" from the firstborn Word called "God/Power" (θεὸς "*Theos*") in a secondary sense. The secondary "God/Power" (θεὸς "*Theos*") was beside/next to (πρὸς *pros* = pertaining to) "THE God" (τὸν θεόν *"TONE Theon"*) in the beginning.

In John 1.1, the Jewish author distinguishes the personified spoken Word/Wisdom from the ultimate God/Power Who created, spoke, or brought it forth in the beginning. Moreover, the Father/Creator gives him the authority to accomplish the Father/Creator's purposes. [cf. Jn. 17.11-12] So, the personified "Word" is called "God/Power" in a subsistent, subservient, and secondary sense. Also, Yeshua, who later embodies the firstborn Word in his life and teachings, is entirely dependent on his Father/Creator for all he is and has.

The Firstborn Word Called "God/Power" Was Beside/Next To "*the* (Most High) God/Power" (Its Creator) in the Beginning

A Christian remarks, " 'And the Word...was...God' John 1:1. Tell me what John is saying here."

John (*YoHanan*) repeats what the Jewish wisdom tradition teaches. Like Philo, *YoHanan* distinguishes between "*ho Theos*" (THE Most High God), Who has no beginning, and Who "no man has ever seen" (1.18) from "*Theos*" (God/Power) whom "the God" brought forth in the beginning. [cf. Fug. 97; Sacr. AC. 9; Som. 1:229-30; Leg. All., II, 86] Many years before YoHanan, Philo taught, "Nothing mortal can be made in the likeness of the Most High, the Father/Creator of the universe, but only in that of the second "God" [i.e., "God" in a secondary sense] who is His *Logos*." [Qu. Gen. II, 62]

Since the human judges and kings in Israel could be called "Gods" (*Eloheem*), the personified Word spoken by the Creator could also be called "God" (*Theos*). [cf. Ex. 21.6; 22.7-9; Ps. 82.6] While the firstborn Word is *not* the Source of Creation, "the [Almighty] God" (*ho Theos*) in the primary sense, he is the expression of the Creator (i.e., "God"/"*Theos*" in a secondary sense). So *YoHannan* writes that *in the beginning,* the firstborn (personified) Word who was called "God" (*Theos*) was beside/next to/associated with "the God" (*ton Theon*), its Creator.

https://www.facebook.com/notes/the-firstborn-word-wisdom-torah/the-word-who-was-power-was-next-to-the-ultimate-sovereign-power-in-the-beginning/213308855362786

https://www.facebook.com/notes/the-firstborn-word-wisdom-torah/this-one-called-god-was-next-to-the-god-in-beginning-1-of-4/364076200286050

A Christian responds, "That IS interesting. A couple of clarifications: John 1:1 literally says, 'the Word was with the God, and God was the Word.' I'm not sure if that ends up changing the meaning in any way, like, God is mentioned as the object of the previous clause and is the subject of the very next one as if John is linguistically connecting the two terms as if they mean the same thing. Maybe not."

The Greek translators of John 1.1 agree that "the Word" instead of "God" is the subject in the clause: "...And the Word was God." In other words, the Word, the spoken expression of *the* God, the Creator, was called "God/Power."

A Christian responds, "As far as the wide agreement among translators that "*Theos*" in the third clause of John 1:1 is not the subject: is it not these same translators who incorrectly - in your view - fail to translate the distinction between *the* God and God in this same verse? Which is it? Are the translators sufficient experts in the language to trust their translation, or aren't they?"

When I refer to "the Greek translators of this text," I have in mind both those who correctly note the distinction here between "*Theos*" (God) and "*ton Theon*" (the God) and those who do not.

A Christian continues, "Now, I want to be clear on this matter, because I have not heard this discussed before. John 1:6 says that John [the baptizer] was sent from God, so you are saying that means John was not sent by THE God, but the lesser God sent him, correct? And when verse 12 says the Word gave to those who accepted Him authority to become children of God, it means that we become children of the lesser God rather than THE God, right? As in, 'the Word gave to those who accepted Him authority to become children of the Word' since there is no definite article? And when verse 13 speaks about those who were not born of flesh or blood but of God, it doesn't mean THE God; it means born of the lesser God? Moreover, when verse 18 says 'no one has seen God', that means no one has seen the lesser God, right...oh wait a minute, that is one of the examples you have given showing the difference between the two Gods... ...Now I'm a little confused. None of these references use the definite article for God, so according to your argument, they should all be referring to the lesser, created Word/God, and yet, especially the last one you say refers to THE God? But if THE God is being referred to in verse 18, even though no definite article is used, how can your argument be that the lack of the definite article in verse 1 means the lesser God is in view?"

In John 1.1-2, the Word called "God/Power" is beside/next to and associated with "the God/the Power," the Creator Who brought it forth in the beginning. The distinction between the single Creator referred to as "the God" (*ton Theon*), and the firstborn Word called "God/Power" (*Theos*) is not made again anywhere else in the book of John. For example, verse 18 of this first chapter does not distinguish between "God/Power" and "the God/the Power." *YoHanan* makes no further distinction between "*Theos*/Power" and "*ton Theon*/the Power" in his book.

A Christian continues, "Additionally, you use Genesis 31:13 from the Septuagint to suggest that the God Jacob encountered at Bethel was not the full, ultimate God, otherwise, THE God would have said they met at 'My place,' or from the Hebrew 'My house'; but Bethel was the name Jacob gave to the place. Jacob made a vow to THE God at Bethel, as attested in the verse, and named the place Bethel in honor of THE God He made the vow to, didn't he? With due respect to Philo, contextually, it seems that God is simply referring to the place Jacob named so that Jacob would know whom He was talking to, right? The vision Jacob had at Bethel was of *HaShem* standing at the top of the ladder, right? And He was afraid because of the vision of *HaShem*, correct? And he made a vow to *HaShem*, true? So then why would he name the place after some other Being, when *HaShem* was the focal point of the whole affair?"

Whatever the original intention of Genesis 31.13 might have been, Philo used this verse as a proof text for a distinction found there between "God" and "the God." Also, since it is well known that "they who are called 'Gods/Powers' are numerous," it is understandable why these Jewish wisdom literature writers would give the title of "God/Power" to the

Creator's firstborn *of* creation, His firstborn, subservient instrument, means, or agent, the personified Wisdom/Word.

The Creator's Word is "spoken," "given birth," or "formed" at the beginning of His way, the foremost (beginning) of His acts of yore, and therefore existed as the beginning of creation (i.e., "when time started"). [cf. Prov. 8.22-31; Rev. 3.14, et cetera.] Also, the author of Hebrews 3.2 writes,"...being faithful to the One *creating* (*poiaysanti* = making) him [i.e., *Osayhu* = his Maker]." However, John 1.1 does not imply that the firstborn *of* God's creation, the personified Word, existed "BEFORE" the beginning of creation. The imperfect tense "was" (ἦν *hain*) expresses the continuous and ongoing existence of the (spoken) Word since the beginning of the Creator's creation...no less and no more.

A Christian responds, "The root for *poiaysanti* has a much different type of meaning for 'to make' then 'to create.' The root also has the meaning of 'to do' or 'making to do.' In the context of Hebrews 3:2, it has to do with making/appointing Yeshua as an apostle and priest in the order of Melchizedek. In John 5:27, it has the meaning of doing/executing judgment. Matthew 20:12 has the root meaning of doing/working in the fields, perhaps bringing forth a harvest. The Greek word often used to speak of creating is '*ktizo*,' not '*poieo*.' '*Poieo*' seems much more about 'making you go to the store' than 'creating you to go to the store.'"

The Greek verb ποιήσαντι (*poiaysanti*) derived from ποιέω (*poieo*) may be translated into English several different ways including "do," "make," "create," "cause," "accomplish," "act," et cetera. In <u>A Greek-English Lexicon of the New Testament</u> by Bauer, Arndt, and Gingrich, the reference to ποιήσαντι (*poiaysanti*) in Hebrews 3.2 is found with the meaning of "God's creative activity (create)."

In Mark 10.6, we read: "But, from (the) beginning of creation (κτίσεως), the God made (ἐποίησεν *epoiaysen*) them male and female." Also, in Acts 17.24 we find, "The God Who made (ποιήσας *poiaysas*) the world and all things in it; being the LORD of heaven and earth, He does not dwell in temples made with hands (χειροποιήτοις)." Similarly, in Rev. 14.7, we read, "...and worship the One Who made (ποιήσαντι *poiaysanti*) the heaven and the earth...."

While the verb (ποιήσαντι) would better be translated in Hebrews 3.2 as "making" (him) rather than "creating" (him), "making" (him) could and should be understood (in this case) as a synonym for "creating" (him). The Creator Who made (ποιήσαντι *poiaysanti*) the heaven and the earth also made (ποιήσαντι) or created and appointed Yeshua to be our delegate (representative) and high priest.

"This One (Called "God/Power") Was Beside/Next To *the* [Most High] God/Power in the Beginning"

A Christian writes, "John, an apostle of Jesus, clearly pointed out that Jesus was God. John 1:1 (NSRV) 'In the beginning was the Word, and the Word was with God, and the Word was God.' "

In John 1.1-2, we read: "In the beginning was the (spoken) Word (i.e., the firstborn Wisdom or Instruction/*Torah*).

And the Word was beside/next to *the* God (τὸν θεόν *ton Theon* = הָאֱלֹהִים *haEloheem* = the Sovereign Power = the single Father/Creator). And the (spoken) Word was [called] "God" (θεὸς *Theos* = אֵל "*El*" = "Power"). This one (called "God/Power") was beside/next to *the* [Most High] God/the Sovereign Power in the beginning." In other words, John writes that the personified first-created Word/Wisdom that Philo had earlier identified as "God/Power" in a secondary sense was beside/next to *the* God/Sovereign Power, its Creator, in the beginning. Consequently, the first-created, firstborn personified Word is *not* "the GOD/Sovereign Power" Who has no beginning or birth.

Trinitarian translators of John 1.1-2 overlook the literal meaning of the Greek verses which distinguish the (spoken) Word called "God" (θεὸς Theos) from "the God" (τὸν θεόν ton Theon) Whom the Word was next to in the beginning. In other words, the Word who was given the title of "God" was not "the God" Whom it was next to in the beginning. The advocates for the three distinct, co-equal, and co-eternal "God-persons" are usually unaware of the alternative understanding for these verses. This Jewish point of view rooted in the wisdom tradition was expressed by Philo of Alexandria many years before John wrote his book.

A generation before *YoHannan* (John) wrote his gospel, Philo taught, "Nothing mortal can be made in the likeness of the Most High One and Father of the universe, but only in that of the second 'God' [i.e., 'God' in a secondary sense], who is His *Logos*." [Qu. Gen. II, 62] And further he explains...to whom God says, 'I am the God, who was seen by you in place of God' [*en topo theou*; Gen. 31.13 LXX]. ...but examine it accurately, and see whether there are really two Gods. For it is said: 'I am the God who was seen by you' not in My place, but 'in place of God' as if he meant some other God. What then should we say? There is *one* true God only, but they who are called 'gods' are numerous. On which account the holy scripture on the present occasion indicates that it is *the* true God that is meant by the use of the article, the expression being, 'I am *the* God (*ho Theos*).' But when the word is used [alternately], it is put without the article with the expression being, 'He who was seen by you in place,' *not* of *the* God (τοῦ θεοῦ *tou Theou*), but simply 'of God' (θεοῦ *Theou*). And what He calls 'God' (without the article) is His chief Word.... [On Dreams, Book 1. 227-230; cf. *Fug*. 97; *Sacr. AC*. 9; Som. 1:229-30; Leg. All., II, 86]

A Christian argues, "All you have is speculation of a mysterious original Jewish milieu extracted from rabbinic theology that was finalized centuries later. During the time of Christ and John, this theology was in a nascent state, and still fighting for dominance. You're attempting to read this later theology into a text that has nothing to do with it."

Not true! The *previous* Jewish background in the Jewish wisdom tradition was *not* "finalized centuries later." The "original Jewish milieu" found in the Jewish wisdom literature, which included Proverbs and Philo's writings, was recorded *before* John wrote his gospel. It is the Trinitarians who attempt to read their much later theology regarding a plural Threesome God into Jewish texts which teach consistently that there is one single Creator alone.

A Christian claims, "There's no evidence that John meant '*Torah*' when he employed the word 'Logos.' Indeed, the Greek text in George Ricker Berry's Interlinear Greek-English New Testament says you're downright wrong. There is a specific Greek word for Law, which is not used here. The Johannine text is specific in saying that the Word is God."

In the Jewish Scriptures, the "Word" *of* God is synonymous with the "Instruction/*Torah*/Law *of* God, *HaShem*. For example, in Isa. 2.3, we read, "...*Torah* (תּוֹרָה) will go forth from *Tzeeyon* (Zion) and the word (*ud'var* וּדְבַר) of *HaShem* (י-ה-ו-ה) from *Y'rushalayeem*." [Micah 4.2; cf. Job 22.22; Ps. 119.17-18] Also, as Philo wrote, "The Law is nothing else but the divine *Logos* prescribing what one should do and prohibiting what one should not do." [De Migratione Abrahami, 130] Consequently, there is no need for "a specific Greek word for Law" to be used in John 1.1-2, since "Word" (דָּבָר *d'var*) is a parallel, synonymous term for the Instruction/*Torah*/Law of *the* God/Sovereign Power.

Note that an *English* translation of the Greek text of John 1.1-3 might only give one literal translation of the Greek "*logos*" as "word." Nevertheless, one should be aware that "*logos*" can also be translated by other words such as "saying, plan, message, account, reason, and teaching/instruction." Furthermore, the Hebrew word for "teaching" or "instruction" is "*torah*," which Jews routinely translated into Greek as "*nomos*/law."

While John 1.1-2 says that the personified Word was called "God/Power," the author (like Philo before him) distinguishes this secondary "God/Power," the derived instrument or means of creation, from "*the* God," the single Source of all things. [cf. Leg. All., II, 86] This subsistent (dependently existing) "God/Power," the first-created, firstborn Word/Wisdom of creation, is pictured as being next to "*the* God/Sovereign Power" Who alone is the only immortal, invisible, unborn Source of all creation, including His firstborn Word. While "*no* man *has ever* seen *the* [Most High] God," many saw the historical human person who embodied "the (spoken) Word" in his life and teachings." [cf. John 1.18]

A Christian responds, "Yes, '*Logos*' does have these meanings...at any rate, the *Logos* is explicitly identified by John as being God."

In Jewish Wisdom literature, the personified "*Logos*," the firstborn, first-created Word/Wisdom *of* the Father/Creator, is given the title of "God/Power." The Word viewed secondarily as "God/Power" is authorized to represent and speak for *the* God/Sovereign Power, Whom it was next to in the beginning.

A Christian responds, "You don't get to have two gods either in Judaism or, despite ignorant claims to the contrary, in Trinitarian Christianity."

In "Trinitarian Christianity," there are three different entities or "persons" who are all identified as being co-equal, co-eternal members of the same "godhead" or unified "pantheon." One of the members of the unified pantheon (i.e., "Godhead") appeared on earth as a visible human being. However, in contrast to the Trinitarian concept of three co-equal god-persons, we find John identifies the single Creator of the Universe as "*the* God" Whom "no man has ever seen." [Jn. 1.18] And, in John 1.1-3, he identifies the first-created Word as being "God/Power" in a subordinate, secondary sense. God's firstborn spoken Word serves its Creator as an instrument of creation like a brush that serves an artist as a means of creating a painting. Neither Philo nor later John portrays the firstborn Word as being a co-equal, co-eternal "God/Sovereign Power." However, Philo and John recognize that "*the* invisible God/Sovereign Power" spoke, gave birth to, or created the firstborn Word/Wisdom, which is secondarily given the title of "God/Power" like Moses, judges, and kings of Israel who are called "Gods/Powers" in

other scriptures. [cf. Ex. 7.1; 21.6; 22.7-9; Deut. 32.43 (DSS); Ps. 97.7; 82.6]

A Christian continues, "Here's what you're writing *into* John: 'In the beginning was the Word. And the Word was with (next to) THE God. And the Word was [called] God.' Here's the wooden translation: "In [the] beginning was the Word, and the Word was with God, and God was the Word."

This deceptive "wooden translation" of John 1.1 hides the distinction which John's Greek text makes between the (spoken) Word, who was "God/Power" and "*the* God/Sovereign Power," which the personified Word was "with" or "next to" in the beginning. Like most other English versions, the "wooden translation" leaves out a definite article ("the" = τὸν "*tone*") in the Greek text before "[*THE*] God (θεόν)." As Philo did a generation earlier, John distinguishes between "*the* God" in the primary and ultimate sense from the Logos, who was referred to as "God" in a derived, secondary sense. By leaving out the definite article, "the" (τὸν "tone"), in English translations, readers are unable to appreciate the distinction John makes between the firstborn Word who was "God/Power" in a secondary sense and "the God/Power" Whom the subordinate "God/Power" was next to in the beginning.

A Christian responds, "Your translation is the same as the J.W.'s, only with a change from an indefinite article insertion to a definite article over-exaggeration which [is] far more unjustified."

The Jehovah's Witnesses may be mistaken regarding their insertion/addition of "an indefinite article" (i.e., "and the Word was [*a*] god/power") in their translation of John 1.1.

But, the Trinitarian translation, which ignores/deletes the *definite* article (i.e., "and the Word was with [*the*] God/Sovereign Power") found in the original Greek text, misleads people into accepting the "far more unjustified" Trinitarian confusion.

A Christian continues, "At any rate, the passage in question is supporting Trinitarianism. On that, I have the scholarship, and you have an amateur hour with ancient texts."

Trinitarian "scholarship" is intent on using pseudo-evidence allegedly found in their misinterpretations of various Jewish texts to support the pagan church fathers' idea of a plural (more than one) "God" with three different personalities or identities. In contrast, the historical evidence for the use of Hebrew and Greek terms should not be ignored. Moreover, the weight of ancient Jewish texts such as Psalms, Proverbs, and later Jewish wisdom literature, including Philo of Alexandria's writings and the rabbinic *midrasheem* to support the idea of a single Father/Creator, *the* God/Sovereign Power, Who has no equals.

A Christian argues, "In Greek, the final clause in John 1.1 is: *'Theos en ho Logos.'* Nothing about 'called' in here. Sorry, John is clear in his meaning. "God was the Word."

John's Jewish understanding of what he wrote in John 1.1 is "non-Trinitarian" and does not support the idea that there is more than one single Father/Creator. What confuses Trinitarian thinkers is an imprecise translation of John 1.1, along with a lack of understanding of the historical Jewish Wisdom literature background. Consequently, Trinitarian translators do not distinguish between "*the* God/Sovereign

Power" and "God/Power," which confuses the readers and influences them to believe that there is more than one single Creator.

Note that Trinitarian translators of John 1.1 ignore the range of meaning and applicability for the title "God" (*"El"*/ *"Eloheem"*/ *"Theos"*) in Jewish Hebrew and later Greek literature. However, it is well known by many scholars of Jewish Scriptures that the title *"Eloheem"* (θεὸς *Theos*) meaning "God/Power" has a range of application. The title "God/Power" is applied not only to *the* Almighty God, the Father/Creator, but also to the first-created Word/Wisdom, and to various human judges and kings. Consequently, the author of John, like the Greek wisdom writer, Philo, before him, made use of the definite article *"the"* to distinguish *the* God (τὸν θεόν *"ton Theon"*), the single Creator, from His firstborn Word who was also called "God" (θεὸς *"Theos"*) on a secondary level. This secondary, derived *"Theos"* (God/Power) was beside/next to (πρὸς *pros*) or secondary to *"TON Theon"* (τὸν θεόν) meaning *"the* God/Sovereign Power" in the beginning.

A Christian continues, "If by employing Philo's definition, your assertion is that John is a Gnostic work, you're very wrong."

Certainly, *if* anyone makes such an assertion, he is clearly mistaken. John's use of a secondary application for the title **"God/*Theos*"** (θεὸς) in John 1.1 includes *no* assertion "that (the book of) John is a Gnostic work."

A Christian continues, "Asimov's Study Guide to Bible p. 964 'The gospel of St. John sets itself firmly against the Gnostic interpretation.' John not only insists on Jesus' divinity, but he also insists on his humanity: John 1:14 (NSRV) 'And the Word became flesh and lived among us...' To be sure, Philo's influence does show up in John, Asimov also points this out, but in the end: John clearly states that Jesus was God."

Asimov is correct that the book of "John sets itself firmly against the Gnostic interpretation." While John's text states that the (spoken) Word was "God," he clearly distinguishes this secondary created "God/Power" from "*the* God/Sovereign Power," its Creator. As John writes, "This one [called "God"] was "with, next to, or beside" *the* God/Sovereign Power in the beginning. [John. 1.2]

A Christian argues, "This is Gnosticism. What you're saying here is that Jesus was a demiurge sent by a distant god to deal with the icky matter."

That is *not* what John 1.1-2 is saying! There is no idea in John 1.1-2 of an infinite chasm between the spirit world and the world of matter, which is regarded as being intrinsically evil. The Jewish Scriptures teach that the Creator's world of creation is "good" rather than "intrinsically evil."

A Christian responds, "You may not explicitly state it, but that is the logical consequence of your theology. '*The* God' didn't want anything to do with creation, so he sent a created demiurge to do the dirty work."

Not only do I *not* explicitly state it, but I also explicitly deny that John considers the Word to be "a demiurge sent by a distant god to deal with the icky matter." The interpretation that "'*the* God' didn't want anything to do with creation, so he sends a created demiurge to do the dirty work," might be "the logical consequence" for some. However, it is not the logical consequence for the author of Proverbs 8 nor any

other Jewish author before or since. On the contrary, Jewish wisdom writers understand that "*the* God/Sovereign Power" Himself creates the world *by* or *through* His firstborn, first-created Word/Wisdom. Credible Jewish authors employ poetic imagery and literary license to picture Wisdom (a.k.a. the Word) as a personified instrument, means, or agent by which the Creator creates the world. In Jewish Wisdom writing, the metaphorical firstborn Word/Wisdom *of* God's creation is never considered to be a "demiurge to do the dirty work."

Note that there is *no* belief expressed in Jewish wisdom writings that would support the gnostic idea that a rebellious Demiurge rather than "*the* God" of Israel created the world. On the contrary, Jewish wisdom tradition views the Creator Himself (rather than an evil demiurge) as creating the "*good*" physical world. Furthermore, Jewish wisdom writers portray the Creator as creating the *good* physical world *by*/*through* His Word/Wisdom, which is considered to be the first of *HaShem*'s creative acts of old. As we read in Proverbs 8.22-31, "ה-ו-ה-י (*HaShem*) acquired/created me (the personified first-created Word/Wisdom, the firstborn *of* creation) at the beginning of His way, the first of His works of old... I was there when He set the heavens in place... Then I was a master craftsman beside/next to Him; and I was daily His delight, one always rejoicing in His presence...."

A Christian responds, "Not all Gnostics attributed evil to the demiurge. Some saw him as good (Plato included) who was confronted with an Ahriman-like creature."

All Gnostics agree that a demiurge, whether good or evil, rather than *the* ultimate God/Sovereign Power, the God of light and goodness, is responsible for the origin and creation of the physical world. In stark contrast to gnostic teaching, the Jewish wisdom writers view the single Father/Creator, *the* God/Sovereign Himself, as being directly responsible for creating this "good" physical world.

A Christian continues, "That's Lady Wisdom, not the Son."

Both the Hebrew personified Wisdom (the first-created lady) and its Greek equivalent, the personified Word (the firstborn son), are viewed as the means or agent/instrument *by/through* which all things are created. The identification of personified "Wisdom" with the personified "Word" as well as "*Torah*/Instruction" of God is ancient. This identification is evident, for example, in the Book of Sirach, when "Wisdom" declares: "Then the Creator of all things gave me a command, and my Creator chose the place for my tent. He said, 'Make your dwelling in Jacob and in Israel receive your inheritance.' Before the ages, in the beginning, He *created* me, and for all the ages, I shall not cease to be. In the holy tent, I ministered before him, and so I was established in Zion. Thus, in the beloved city, He gave me a resting place, and in Jerusalem was my domain. I took root in an honored people, in the portion of the LORD, His heritage. ...Whoever obeys me will not be put to shame, and those who work with me will not sin." Then Sirach adds, "All this is the book of the covenant of the Most High God, the *Torah* that Moses commanded us as an inheritance for the congregations of Jacob." [29.8-23; see also L. Ginzberg, "*Perusheem veHiddusheem beeY'rushalmee*," IV, 1961, p. 20]

As Ephraim Urbach writes in his book _The Sages_ [pp 198-99]: Rabbi *Hosha'ai* expounded the verse in Proverbs thus: "'*Amon – Uman*' [artisan or architect]; the *Torah* says: 'I was the instrument of the Holy One, blessed be He.' As a rule, when a human king builds a palace, he does not build

it by himself but calls in an architect, and the architect does not plan the building in his head, but he makes use of rolls and tablets, to know how to make the rooms and wickets. Even so, the Holy One, blessed be He, looked in the *Torah* and created the world. And the *Torah* declares, "With '*resheet*' [E.V. 'In the beginning'] God created, and '*resheet*' means none other than *Torah* [*HaShem*'s Word or Instruction], as it is said 'The LORD made me '*resheet*' [E.V. 'as the beginning'] of His way.'" [Gen. Rabbah i, 1, p. 2] Further, Rabbi Akiva refers to the *Torah* as "the precious instrument by which the world was created." [*Avot* 3.14]

A Christian responds, "Couldn't give a damn what Rabbi anyone has to say when interpreting Christian theology just as they don't give a damn what we have to say regarding Jewish theology. This has nothing to do with Christianity."

Rabbi *Hosha'ai* is *not* "interpreting Christian theology." Instead, he is expounding on Proverbs 8.22 as it is understood in the non-Trinitarian Jewish tradition long before the pagan church fathers invented the later Trinitarian perversion: "The LORD (*HaShem*) acquired/made me at the beginning of His way." Rabbi *Hosha'a*i and other Jewish wisdom writers picture the personified Word/Wisdom as being next to its God, the ultimate Sovereign Power, in the beginning. This Jewish point of view "has nothing to do with (later Trinitarian) Christianity," which deifies "the Word" found in John 1.1-3 and throughout the rest of the book as a "co-equal, co-eternal" God-person.

A Christian argues, "OK. But you have to do better if you're going to overturn 2,000 years of [Trinitarian] writing and scholarship on the issue."

To uphold later Trinitarian writing and scholarship, which is contradictory to Jewish thought, one would first have to prove that John 1.1-3 does not distinguish the (spoken) Word, which was "God/Power," from "*the* God," the ultimate "Sovereign Power," Whom the Word was with/next to in the beginning. Only then would Trinitarian "scholarship" be able to overturn the original Jewish meaning of John 1.1-3 written almost 2,000 years ago.

A Christian responds, "I did, which you're blithely ignoring to create your own special heresy which in fact is simply a rerun of the same stunt Arius pulled."

While many Christians consider the polytheistic Gentiles, Athanasius, and the church fathers to be their spiritual mentors, I do not regard their Christian opponent, Arius, to be my authority. Athanasius and company equate the visible, mortal, and human god, "Jesus," with the Father/Creator, which is an aberration imposed on John 1.1-3 and other Jewish texts. John's "*Logos*" can only be properly understood in its original Jewish context within the Jewish wisdom tradition. The later Trinitarian interpretation of John's *Logos* (Word) has no root in the Jewish wisdom tradition. This ignorance was evident at the council of Nicaea in 325 C.E., which was led by pagan church fathers, including Alexander of Alexandria and Athanasius. Jews familiar with the Jewish wisdom tradition were not invited to this defining council.

The One Single Supreme Almighty Power/God, the Father/Creator, and Various Dependent Powers/Gods

In John 1.1-3, the personified Word, which was called "God/Power" (*El*), was with/next to *the* Most High God (*haEloheem*) Who spoke, bore, brought forth, or created the personified Word in the beginning. In order to properly understand what it means to call the firstborn Word "Power" (*El*), one must first understand that various powerful rulers, including judges and kings, were called "God/Power" in the Hebrew Scriptures. These mortal "Gods/Powers" are not considered to be equal to or the same as the Most High "God" Who is the sole Source of all that exists.

A Christian responds, "That would go against all principles of there being one God. The Word is God's spoken Word that He spoke into existence His coming in flesh through the Son/person/image of God. His image and not another."

There is only one single supreme Almighty Power/God (*haEloheem*), the Father/Creator. However, there are many secondary dependent "Powers" (*Eloheem*). Many non-Hebrew speakers are unaware of the fact that various kings, judges, and messengers are referred to as "*Eloheem*" (Powers/Gods) in the Hebrew Scriptures. Calling the (spoken) Word "Power" or "God" in a secondary sense does not negate the fact that there is ultimately only one Most High God Who has no equals. As Yeshua stated, "the Father is greater than I." [John 10.29; 14.28]

A Christian responds, "The Father, of course, is greater, because He humbled Himself. He took on flesh, and flesh is not greater than His Spirit. His Spirit; His glory fills eternity."

Paul says that Yeshua who was created in God's image/form, humbled himself in obedience to his Creator/Father. [Phil. 2.1-11] We are never told that "the

Father humbled Himself" to anyone. The visible, mortal Yeshua represents the invisible, immortal Creator/Maker. The human Yeshua did not grasp for equality with God, his (metaphorical) Father, as Adam and Eve, the first humans, did.

A Christian continues, "John 3:12-13

12 If I have told you earthly things, and ye believe not, how shall ye believe, if I tell you of heavenly things?

13 And no man hath ascended up to heaven, but he that came down from heaven, even the Son of man which is in heaven."

First, note that the last phrase "who/which is in heaven" found at the end of verse 13 in some English versions is absent in the most reliable older Greek manuscripts. So, in John 3.13, we read, "And no one has ascended into heaven, but He who descended from heaven, even the Son of Man." (NAS) Secondly, in John 3.13, the author refers to "the son of Man/Adam" and not to "the Creator of Man/Adam." Thirdly, Yeshua is viewed in John 3.13 as the human being who "came down from Heaven/God" (i.e., a human creature with human parents sent by the Creator) to be the Almighty God's representative human redeemer, king, judge, and prophet. Yeshua, the human son of Joseph, like all human prophets, was sent by God or descended from Heaven (i.e., from God) to speak the words of God.

A Christian continues, "1 Corinthians 12:3--Wherefore I give you to understand, that no man speaking by the Spirit of God calleth Jesus accursed: and that no man can say that Jesus is the Lord but by the Holy Ghost."

Yeshua is the human Master/Lord and *HaShem*'s anointed King who was sent by the "one God and Father of all, who is above all, and through all, and in you all." [Eph. 4.5-6] Yeshua is not the "one God and Father of all, Who is above all (including our Master Yeshua)."

A Christian continues, "Rev. 17:14--JESUS is not just Lord. He is the LORD of Lords."

Yeshua is the human Master/Lord of all human Master/Lords. However, this temporary human Master/Lord Yeshua is the metaphorical servant/son of the Most High God, the Father/Creator, Whom he worships and serves.

A Christian continues, "Phil. 2:10-11--Every knee shall bow, every tongue shall confess He is Lord, to the glory of the Father."

Every knee shall bow and every tongue shall confess that Yeshua is Master/Lord, to the glory of the Father/Creator Who is greater than Yeshua.

A Christian continues, "Isaiah 42:8--His glory will He not give to another."

God, the Father/Creator, does not give His glory to another, including Yeshua, the firstborn faithfully obedient son among many faithfully obedient siblings.

The Mortal Human Power/God and the Most High Power/God He Worships

When Yeshua says, "I and the Father are one," do you think that he means that he (the son) is one with the Father/Creator or that he (the son) is the Father/Creator? When a wife says that she and her husband are one, does she mean I am one with my husband or that she is her husband?

A Christian argues, "Is a husband in a wife and a wife in her husband? No. Then they are not one like Father and Son since JESUS is God who was manifest in the flesh, not two separate persons, but He Himself took on flesh. This is written in scripture. The flesh was His veil, made in the likeness of sinful flesh, condemned sin in the flesh."

The firstborn Word of God (not the Father/Creator) Who spoke the Word, took on flesh. Also, many human creatures are called "*El*" (Powerful Ruler) or "*Eloheem*" (Powerful Rulers). However, this does not mean that any of these mortal human creatures were the Most High *Eloheem* Who has no human equal(s).

A Christian responds, "There was no one like JESUS CHRIST. Not even close. Name me one person who laid their life down for the world? One who performed the miracles JESUS did?"

Yeshua is a mortal human creature who is called "*El*" (Power) like other mortal human rulers are called "*Eloheem*" (Powerful Rulers). [cf. Psalm 82.6; John 10.34] The visible, mortal Yeshua worships and serves the invisible, immortal Most High *Eloheem* (the Father/Creator) Who is greater than him. [John 10.29; 14.28] While Yeshua is the human King of Kings and Lord

of Lords, this human King/Lord is not one like (or equal to) the All-Powerful *Eloheem* Whom he worships and serves, not even close. The human Yeshua, who models faithful obedience to the Creator, is the firstborn among many human siblings who are also faithfully obedient to God. Yeshua is not the Creator/Father/Maker.

The Creator's Firstborn Word/Wisdom/*Torah* Was the Instrument/Means *through/by* Which the Almighty Created All Things

Someone remarks, "There's only one thing I don't understand. What do you say about the Word being the single Creator's subservient agent of creation...not the co-creator identified in John 1? To me, the Word is the Creator's Word, so it must be part of Him just as our word is part of us."

Jewish wisdom literature portrays the firstborn, first-created Word/Wisdom as being "born" or "created" as a separate identity from the single Father/Creator before everything else is created. According to Sephardic Jewish theologian, *RaMBaM*/Maimonides (1135/38-1204 CE), "This God (the Father/Creator) is One, not two or more than two, but One whose unity is different from all other unities that there are. He is not one as a genus, which contains many species, is one. Nor is He one as a body, containing parts and dimensions, is one. However, His (God's) is a unity/oneness that which there is no other anywhere. (*Yad, Yesode HaTorah* 1:7)" In other words, the oneness of the single Father/Creator is considered to be one indivisible whole without any parts, partners, co-equals, or co-eternals.

While our words do come directly from our minds, they still have a distinct, subsistent (dependently existing), and subservient relationship to our minds. In other words, the firstborn, personified Word identified in John 1.1-3 is dependent on the One Who spoke it or brought it into existence and should not be considered to be a co-equal, co-eternal, "co-creator." By way of example, when an artist uses a paintbrush or paint as a means by which to create a picture/painting, no one would consider the dependent brush or paint in his or her hand (the artist's instrument or means) to be "a co-artist."

The *from* Whom and the *through* Whom Are All Things

Jewish wisdom literature (including John) portrays the personified Word/Wisdom as the firstborn, first-created agent of creation. At the same time, *HaShem*, the Father/Creator, is the single Source of all creation, including His Word/Wisdom.

A Christian responds, "No. This sounds exactly like something my Jehovah's Witness father might say. Consider, please, these two passages:
OF THE SON: 'For by him were all things created, that are in heaven, and that are in earth, visible and invisible, whether they be thrones, or dominions, or principalities, or powers: all things were created by him, and for him.' (Col 1:16).
OF THE FATHER: 'Thou art worthy, O Lord, to receive glory and honor and power: for thou hast created all things, and for thy pleasure, they are and were created.' (Rev 4:11)"

These two passages illustrate the distinction between the Father/Creator and the firstborn, first-created Word/Wisdom. In Col. 1.16, we read that all things were created *by means of/through* him (Yeshua, who embodies the (spoken) Word/Wisdom in his life, works, and teachings), *not FROM* Him (the single Father/Creator). In other words, the firstborn Word is the created instrument/means or agent, not the source of creation. In Rev. 4.11, we find that *HaShem* (*Adonai*), the single Father/Creator created all things. He *alone* is the source of all creation. As Paul writes in 1 Cor. 8.6: "Yet for us, there is *one* God (*Eloheem*), the Father, *FROM* Whom are all things....and *one* Master/Lord (*Adon/Mar*), Yeshua the Messiah (who embodies the Word/Wisdom in his life, works, and teachings), *THROUGH* or *FOR* whom are all things."

Throughout the Renewed Covenant Scriptures, the firstborn, first-created Word/Wisdom is always viewed as the *THROUGH* whom or the *BY* whom (i.e., the instrument/means) are all things and *never* as the *FROM* Whom (i.e., the single Source) are all things. The critical distinction between the firstborn Word/Wisdom and the Father/Creator is missed by many. For Paul and others, there is only One *FROM* Whom are all things, one single God, the Father/Creator, the Source of creation including His Word/Wisdom. Moreover, there is one subsistent (dependently existing) and subservient Word/Wisdom, the instrument/means or agent of creation, *THROUGH* whom are all things. For example, while the paint is the means by which an artist paints a picture, it is not a second artist. Likewise, while the personified first-created, firstborn Word/Wisdom is the means by which the Creator made all things, it is not a second creator.

A Christian responds, "One of my points is that both passages speak of the creation of *all* things by the Son and the Father, respectively. This demands that Jesus is pre-existent. The other point is that creation is *for* both the Father and the Son."

The Jewish Scriptures testify that the single Father/Creator created all things through or by *means of* His personified firstborn, first-created Word/Wisdom in the beginning. Furthermore, according to *YoHanan* (John) 1.1-14, the personified firstborn Word/Wisdom *later* became embodied in the life and teachings of Yeshua, the patrilineal son of David. However, the visible, historical Yeshua did *not* exist either at the time of creation. While the personified Word/Wisdom was with its Creator in the beginning, it did not become embodied in the life and teachings of the historical Yeshua until a much later time in human history.

Section Three: "And the (Spoken) Word Became Flesh…"

Philo: "…the King (i.e., the Messiah) Is a Living *Torah*/Law…"

A Christian notes, "I'm skeptical of the "*Torah* incarnate" idea because John 1:17 (and other passages in the 4th Gospel) put Jesus in a certain opposition to "the Law."

Most Christian translations of *YoHanan* (John) 1.17 and other seemingly similar passages in the 4th Gospel insert "a certain opposition to the Law" in their poor, misleading translations. However, no such opposition was meant or intended in John 1.17 or any other seemingly similar passage in John. In fact, throughout the whole book of *YoHanan*, Yeshua is portrayed as the actualization of the grace and truth of God's Instruction/Word (*Torah*/Logos), which all *HaShem*'s people should endeavor to realize in their lives.

A Christian elaborates, "... John 1:17 says ... "the Law was given by Moses, grace and truth came through Jesus Christ." That is a theme developed throughout the rest of the book."

Since most Christians misunderstand *YoHanan* 1.17, they say that the Law is oppositional to the grace and truth that came through Yeshua. However, one should understand that just as *HaShem* gave His *Torah*/Law through Moses, so also, He sent Yeshua to actualize the grace and truth of the *Torah*/Law in his life and teachings. As Philo points out a generation earlier, "… the King (i.e., the Messiah) is at once a living *Torah*/Law (νόμος ἔμψυχος *nomos empsychos*

like Moses), and the *Torah*/Law is a just King." [2 On the Life of Moses I, 4]

A Christian responds, "...Jesus was opposed to Moses or the keeping of the Law. ...the point of the 4th Gospel is not that Jesus 'lived out *Torah*.'"

While the traditional, famous Christian (counterfeit) "Jesus was (and is) opposed to Moses, and the keeping of the Law," the so-called "4th Gospel" portrays the original Jewish Yeshua as *HaShem*'s Instruction/Word being embodied in Yeshua's life and teachings.

A Christian responds, "I don't think that is a correct way of understanding the language in the 4th Gospel. The idea of 'embodied' is not there."

When John writes that *HaShem*'s abstract (personified) Word/Wisdom, which was called "God/Power," was next to "the God (its Creator)" in the beginning, he echoes earlier Jewish Wisdom literature. The Instruction/Word the Father/Creator transmitted to Moses contains the grace and truth for all the people of Israel to apply to their lives. Many years later, in the introduction to John's wisdom book, we read that the Father's Instruction/Word "became flesh." Subsequently, throughout his book, John portrays Yeshua as the embodiment of the loving-kindness (grace) and truth of *HaShem*'s Instruction/Word. In other words, Yeshua metaphorically embodied in his life and teachings the Creator's Instruction/Word, which expresses His loving-kindness and truth.

A Christian adds, "Jn 1:17 ὅτι ὁ νόμος διὰ Μωσέως ἐδόθη ἡ χάρις καὶ ἡ ἀλήθεια διὰ Ἰησοῦ Χριστοῦ ἐγένετο. 'For the law

was given by Moses, but grace and truth came by Jesus Christ.'
is a very good translation. I ought to just block you as a
worthless know-nothing."

**There is no Greek conjunction in John 1.17 that expresses
"*but*" or opposition between "the law..." and "grace and
truth...." So, inserting the word '*but*" creates an unfortunate
and misleading translation. An accurate translation reads,
"For the *Torah*/Law was given by *Moshe* (Moses); the
loving-kindness (grace) and truth came through Yeshua, the
Messiah." In other words, Yeshua revealed/demonstrated
the loving-kindness (grace) and the truth of *HaShem*'s
Torah/Law.**

https://articles.etrfi.info/?p=131

The Abstract Personified "Word" Becomes Embodied in Yeshua's Life and Teachings

Someone comments, "You talk of Yeshua as if he came into
existence as a being circa 4BC. I claim he was the first-created
being, one of the Sons of God."

**The abstract/nonconcrete firstborn, first-created
personified Word (by means of or through which God
created all things) became embodied in the life and
teachings of the historical Yeshua long after creation.**

Someone asks, "Who was 'the Word' before he took on a
physical existence? Personification attributes human qualities to

inanimate objects. Was he an inanimate object, a philosophical concept, a disembodied emotion?"

"Personification" attributes human qualities to both visible objects and abstract nouns/concepts such as God's spoken "word." The word/command by means of or through which the Creator created the universe was originally introduced in Genesis as a verb (i.e., *"Eloheem said*, 'Be light!'"). [Genesis 1.3] **Later, God's word/command was referred to in the Psalms as a noun (i.e., "by the *word* of *HaShem* (-ו-ה-י ה) the heavens were made…").** [Psalm 33.6] **Subsequently, Jewish Wisdom literature pictured God's word/command as being the Creator's personified Word/Wisdom. [Proverbs 8.22-31; Wisdom 1.4-9; 24.3, 8-9; Sirach 29.8-23; _Leg. All._ III. 175; _Agr._ 51; _Confl._ 146; John 1.1-3]**

Someone remarks and asks, "My words become a reality when I follow through on a promise. Is this what God did with respect to Yeshua? If this is what you mean, Yeshua has no existence as a being before his conception as a human being."

Yes, the personified abstract firstborn, first-created Word/Wisdom pictured as being with or next to its Creator in the beginning, later became embodied in the reality of Yeshua's life and teachings. The same Word can become embodied in the life and teachings of all those who emulate Yeshua's life and teaching. In other words, God's Word becomes a reality in the life and teachings of all those who are "in the Messiah," as Paul taught. [cf. Romans 8.1; 2 Cor. 2.14; 5.17; etc.]

Someone responds, "Yeshua claimed a personal pre-existence. Ignoring this cannot negate it. It must be dealt with."

Again, the personified firstborn Word/Wisdom, which was beside/next to its Creator, in the beginning, did not physically or literally (pre)exist as a literal visible, mortal human creature. In other words, while God's personified and invisible (spoken) Word/Wisdom existed at the beginning of time, the later visible and historical Yeshua who embodied the (spoken) Word in his life and teachings did not yet exist.

In *YoHanan* (John) 17.5, 24, we read, "Now, Father/Creator glorify/honor me (Yeshua) in Your presence with the glory/honor which I (who embodies your firstborn Word) was (destined) to have in Your presence before the world existed…. Father, I desire that they whom You gave me may also be with me where I am, to behold my glory which You have given me in Your love for me before the foundation of the world." Note that the visible human Yeshua did not physically exist as a mortal person with Jewish parents when God created the world. Instead, it was the abstract personified firstborn/first-created Word, which Yeshua embodied in his life and teachings that existed in God's presence at the beginning when He (the Father/Creator created the world.

Note that in *YoHanan* 17.5, 24, the historical, human Yeshua who embodies the firstborn/first-created Word/Wisdom in his life and teachings requests that he be glorified/honored with the glory/honor, which he was destined to have in his Father's/Creator's presence even "before the world existed." Yeshua did not literally or physically exist as a finite, mortal human person with Jewish parents before God created the world. Instead, the abstract personified firstborn Word metaphorically existed in the presence of God before it was embodied in Yeshua's actual life and teachings.

The "Word" Embodied in the Life and Teachings of Yeshua

In the Greek text for John 8.58, Yeshua says, "I am [he, the Son of Man or the Word] before *Avraham* was born." Furthermore, in the next chapter, the man who is born blind says, "I am [he, the one who used to sit and beg]." [9.9] There is *no* reason to capitalize "AM" in either of these two contexts.

In Jewish wisdom literature, the Creator's "Word" or "Wisdom" is personified (i.e., referred to *as if* it was a person who existed at the beginning next to God) long before Yeshua was born. Jewish writers and interpreters understand that the (spoken) Word/Wisdom, which is pictured as being next to its Creator in the beginning, is a literary personification and is *not* considered to be a historical person who existed before *Avraham*, *Moshe*, and later Yeshua was born.

Personifications of abstract notions like the "word" or "wisdom" and the "evil inclination" may be referred to by pronouns like "I," "me," "you," "she," "he," "his," "her," "who," or "they." For example, as we read in Proverbs 7.4-27, "Say to Wisdom, '*You* are my sister,' and call Understanding, 'a friend.' *They* (Wisdom and Understanding) may safeguard you from a forbidden woman (i.e., alluring Wickedness, tempting Foolishness, or the Evil Inclination), from a strange woman who makes *her* words glib. ...Do not incline your heart to *her* ways; do not stray in *her* pathways. For *she* has felled many victims; the number of *her* slain is many. Her house is the way to the grave, descending to the chambers of death."

YoHanan (John) identifies Yeshua as the personified Word, which was beside/next to its Creator "before *Avraham* was born." In other words, the personified Word/Wisdom beside/next to its Creator, in the beginning, became embodied in the life and teachings of the human historical person, Yeshua, who lived on earth long after the completion of creation.

The Spoken Firstborn Word (*Not* the Invisible Creator) Became Flesh (i.e., a Visible, Mortal Man)

The Creator is not contained in a bush or a temple or one of His creatures/sons. Also, no one should worship any visible bush, temple, or mortal human so

A Christian asks, "But doesn't John chapter one identify Yeshua as being the incarnate form of the immortal Creator?"

No, John chapter one does *not* identify Yeshua "as being the incarnate form of the immortal Creator." Instead, John identifies Yeshua as one who embodies the personified Word/Wisdom in his life and teachings. Jewish writers understand that the firstborn, first-created Word/Wisdom, rather than the later historical Yeshua, is beside/next to the immortal/eternal Creator (*the* God/Sovereign Power) in the

beginning. While the personified Word/Wisdom is given God's authority or title, "God/Power," in John 1.1-3, the firstborn Word/Wisdom is *not* considered to be a second co-equal, co-eternal God/Sovereign Power/Creator.

===

A Christian remarks, "You are basically stating that it is impossible for the Eternal God to (have) stepped out of eternity & into time because if He did, He would have ceased being the Eternal One."

While *YoHanan* (John), a Jewish wisdom writer, wrote that "the firstborn Word became flesh," he did not say that the Eternal God Who spoke or brought forth the Word, in the beginning, became visible, mortal flesh.

To prove Jesus is God, a Christian quotes Colossians 1.15-18, "& this is why He will have 'PREEMINENCE' in ALL things. (15) He is the IMAGE of the INVISIBLE God, the firstborn over ALL creation. (16) For BY Him ALL things were CREATED that are in heaven & that are on earth, VISIBLE & INVISIBLE, whether thrones or dominions or principalities or powers. All things were CREATED THROUGH Him & FOR Him. (17) And He is BEFORE ALL things, & IN Him ALL things CONSIST. (18) And He is the HEAD of the body, the church, who is the beginning, the FIRSTBORN from the DEAD, that in ALL THINGS He may have the PREEMINENCE."

When John and Paul portray Yeshua as the firstborn, first-created Word, the instrument or means of creation through which "ALL things were CREATED," they do not mean that this historical person born to Joseph and Mary was visibly present at the creation. Instead, they are indicating

that Yeshua embodies the firstborn Word/Wisdom of God in his life and teachings.

While Yeshua is the ideal human IMAGE of the INVISIBLE God, he is *not* the INVISIBLE God. Also, the sole Creator/Father, the Most High God Whom Yeshua worships and serves, is never portrayed as being either the "FIRSTBORN of creation" or "FIRSTBORN from the DEAD." So, Paul writes, "And, he (Yeshua) is the HEAD of the body, the assembly, who is the ruling head, FIRSTBORN from the DEAD, that in ALL THINGS he might become first."

Man/Adam was created in the IMAGE of the INVISIBLE God. Yeshua is the second Man/Adam who lived up to that image or design of God as the Creator intends the rest of us to do. Again, while Yeshua represents the immortal, invisible Father/Creator, he is *not* the INVISIBLE God Himself.

"As *Moshe* Lifted Up the Serpent in the Wilderness, Even So, Must the Son of Man Be Lifted Up..." [John 3.14-15]

A Jew writes, "'Nachash' has the same gematria as 'Messiah,' and, according to Christian scripture (John 3:14) and Jewish aggadah, was identified as one and the same."

Yes, both of the Hebrew words "*nachash*" (נָחָשׁ) and "*MasheeaH*" (מָשִׁיחַ) equal 358. In John 3.14-15, we read, "As *Moshe* lifted up the serpent in the wilderness, even so, must the Son of Man be lifted up. That whosoever believes in him should not perish, but have eternal life." And, in Isaiah 14.29, we read, "Rejoice not, all you Philistines, that the rod/staff that struck (beat) you have been broken. From the root of a snake (נָחָשׁ *naHash*) shall emanate/come forth a viper (צֶפַע *tzpha*), and his progeny or deeds/fruit (וּפִרְיוֹ *upheero*) will be like those of a flying/fiery serpent (שָׂרָף מְעוֹפֵף *saraph m' opheph*)." | אַל־תִּשְׂמְחִי פְלֶשֶׁת כֻּלֵּךְ כִּי נִשְׁבַּר

[שֵׁבֶט מַכֵּךְ כִּי־מִשֹּׁרֶשׁ נָחָשׁ יֵצֵא צֶפַע וּפִרְיוֹ שָׂרָף מְעוֹפֵף:

Radak explains that "King Uzziah had fought the Philistines and defeated them -- see 2 Chronicles 26.6. After he died and was ultimately succeeded by the wicked *AHaz*, the Philistines rebelled, invaded Judah's lowlands, and regained control. Now that King *AHaz* had died, Isaiah warns the Philistines that although the staff [of King Uzziah] who had beaten them had been broken during the reign of the wicked king (*AHaz*), they should not rejoice. For from the root of the snake will emerge a viper (*HaShem's* Messiah/Hezekiah) whose deeds will be like those of a flying/fiery serpent) who will deal them a severe blow." [Also, keep in mind that the later "Son of Man," Yeshua *ben Yoseph*, was Hezekiah's progeny.]

==

This passage reminds us that many "Palestinians" rejoiced when the rod/staff that struck Egypt and Jordan (in 1967) was broken in 2005. Even though Sharon and company uprooted *Torah*
believers from the "Gaza strip," today's Philistines should not rejoice that the rod/staff that beat them in 1967 was broken by Sharon's non-believing Israeli government. There is coming a day when *HaShem* will
return *Torah* observant people to their homes in the area.

It should be evident to everyone (including Bush, Obama, and the Israelis today) that those who refuse to live in peace with their Jewish neighbors who live nearby will not live in harmony with these neighbors just because they have been forced to move further away.
https://ladderofjacob.com/2014/10/06/holysnake/

The Son of Man Who Descended from Heaven/God

The visible, mortal Yeshua does *not* descend from the heavens as a non-human extraterrestrial. Instead, he is an earthly human being who is conceived, born, and raised by human parents. Also, he participates in life like every other human creature. Like everyone else, Yeshua is tempted in every way and learns obedience to his Creator by what he suffers. [Hebrews 4.15; 5.7-8]

A Christian objects, "He came from heaven above:

John 3:13 'And no man hath ascended up to heaven, but he that came down from heaven, even the Son of man which is in heaven.'

"John 6:33 'For the bread of God is he which cometh down from heaven, and giveth life unto the world.'

John 6.38 'For I came down from heaven, not to do my own will, but the will of Him that sent me.'"

First, note that some English versions of John 3.13 (like the one quoted above) add the phrase "who/which is in heaven" at the end of the verse. These words are absent in

the most reliable older Greek manuscripts. John 3.13 should read as "And no one has ascended into heaven, but He who descended from heaven, even the Son of Man." (NAS) Secondly, notice that in John 3.13, the author refers to "the son of Man/Adam" and not to "the Creator of Man/Adam" as one who came down from Heaven/God. Thirdly, Yeshua is viewed in John 3.13 as a human being (i.e., a human creature with human parents and not as a non-human being) who "came down from Heaven/God." In other words, Heaven, a circumlocution for God, the Father/Creator, sent Yeshua like all other true human prophets, to communicate His word/instruction to the rest of humanity.

A Christian argues, "Yeshua is the only one to come down from heaven. If we use your logic, then all mankind came down from heaven. But that is not what scripture says."

Again, Heaven (a.k.a. the Father/Creator) sends human servants to communicate His word/message to others. Furthermore, remember that other true prophets besides Yeshua were also sent down from Heaven/God, the Father/Creator. [Ex. 3.14, 4.28, 5.22; Isa. 48.16, 61.1; Jer. 25.4; Hag. 1.12; Zech. 2.8, John 1.6, et cetera]

Note that unlike Yeshua and the prophets, the single God, the Father/Creator, is not sent by anyone, and He does not come down or go anywhere. As Paul said, "The God Who made the world and everything in it is the MASTER/LORD of heaven and earth and does not live in temples made by hands. Moreover, He is not served by human hands as if he needed anything. Since He Himself gives all people (including Yeshua and the other prophets) life and breath... For in Him (the only true God) we live and move and exist...." [Acts 17.24-28]

A Christian counters, "Not all instances of the word heaven imply God. God created the heavens too. Does this mean God created the gods? Your argument has no weight."

Yes, God created the heavens and the earth. I just quoted Paul, where he spoke about "the God" Who "is the MASTER/LORD of heaven and earth." Obviously, "not all instances of the word 'Heaven' imply God." However, "Heaven" is often used in Jewish literature as an indirect way of referring to the Creator, the single Source of all that exists.

A Christian responds, "The three passages I cited (John 3:13, John 6.33, and John 6.38) you 'know' (argue) refer to God, when in fact, they don't."

In John 3.13, does "the son of Adam" who descended from Heaven come down from a created *place* (heaven), or was he sent down from the God Who created the heavens and the earth?

In John 6.33, does "the bread/word of God" which gives life unto the world come down from a created *place* (heaven) or does "the bread/word of God" which gives life unto the world come directly from the God Who created the heavens and the earth?

In John 6.38, does the word/messenger of God that does the will of the God Who sent him come down from a created *place* (heaven) or does the word of God that does the will of the God that sent him to come directly from the God Who created the heavens and the earth?

The Personified Spoken Word Becomes Embodied in the Life and Teachings of a Historical Person, Yeshua

A Christian claims, "What the Apostles did was recognize that Jesus Christ is a *person*, not an abstraction. The Sages and others may have caught a glimpse of the truth, but Jesus *is* Truth. This is revealed by the Father."

Yes, Yeshua, the anointed king, is very much a real historical person rather than an abstraction. He was a real human creature like the rest of us. Like Pilate, the Roman executioner, said, "Behold! The man!" Since the historical Yeshua embodies the firstborn, first-created Word/Wisdom in his life and teachings, he is characterized metaphorically as being the Word (i.e., *HaShem*'s Instruction/*Torah*/Law or "the Way, the Truth, and the Life)." [cf. John 1.1-14; 14.6]

A Christian responds, "My point is that the Lord Jesus is and has *always* been a person. From before time."

The spoken *personified* Word, not the historical person, Yeshua, was with or next to its Creator in the beginning when time began. In other words, the historical person, Yeshua, did *not* exist before he was conceived and born long after creation was completed. When *YoHanan* (John) characterizes the later historical Yeshua metaphorically as the personified Word, which "becomes flesh and dwells among us" (John 1.14), he understands that Yeshua embodies the (spoken) Word/Wisdom or Instruction/Law in his life and teachings. Just as we might characterize some today as "a walking dictionary," *YoHanan* pictures Yeshua as being "the living, breathing Word/*Logos*/*Torah*."

There is *no* evidence in Jewish wisdom literature for a real, historical human being who preexisted. Instead, when John, a Jewish wisdom author, identifies the human Yeshua metaphorically as "the (spoken) Word/Wisdom that becomes flesh" (cf. John 1.14), he understands that Yeshua embodies the personified first-created Word/Wisdom in his life and teachings. However, while the human Yeshua was in the thoughts/plans of the Father/Creator, the historical Yeshua did not exist in a physical human form at the beginning of creation before he was born in historical time. Also, saying that "the (spoken) Word became flesh" means that "the Word became a man who was a visible, mortal human creature who was nothing but a man."

The Spoken Personified Word (Present at Creation) Was Embodied in the Visible Human Yeshua Later in History

At the beginning of creation, the spoken firstborn Word was with/next to its Creator. However, it had not yet become embodied in the life and teachings of Yeshua, the later historical person with Jewish parents.

A Christian counters, "Sir, the Scriptures don't say 'not yet become flesh in the life and teachings.' (John 1:14) 'And the Word was made flesh, and dwelt among us, (and we beheld his glory, the glory as of the only begotten of the Father), full of grace and truth.' Not 'in the life and teachings' (of Yeshua).'"

When the Jewish wisdom author states in John 1.14, "And the Word was made flesh and dwelt among us," he is expressing the idea that the personified firstborn/first-created Word/Wisdom became embodied in the life and teachings of Yeshua.

A Christian responds, "Since Yeshua is the Word, surely then the Word is walking visibly. Yeshua is the Word, and there remains no doubt HE exhibited what HE is. Yeshua and the Word are not two different things to imbibe in life or teaching."

The historical human Yeshua with Jewish parents and brothers and sisters was not "walking visibly" as a human creature in the beginning when the metaphorical personified Word/Wisdom was created.

A Christian answers, "Yes, the Word was walking visibly. Otherwise, you will have to admit the FATHER is visible."

The idea that the personified firstborn, first-created Word/Wisdom which the Creator spoke, in the beginning, was already visible, mortal flesh before the world was created makes no sense.

The Source/Creator/FATHER of all that exists and His firstborn Word/Wisdom by which He created all that exists were invisible at the beginning of creation. The first-created Word/Wisdom did not become "walking visible" flesh in the life and teachings of Yeshua until much later in human history.

A Christian responds, "I never said visible flesh, I only said visible."

A visible person who walks and talks like the mortal, human Yeshua is a person of flesh and bone.

A Christian asks, "Are angels of flesh and bone?"

Yes, angels/messengers sent by God were created beings who appear in the form "of flesh and bone." Take a look at the messengers recorded in the Hebrew Scriptures. Three of them partook of a feast with *Avraham*. [Gen. 18] One of them had a wrestling match with *Yaakov*. [Gen. 32]

A Christian asks, "Were they (the angels) human?"

In the Hebrew Scriptures, angels/messengers were referred to as though they were human. However, what do these questions regarding God's visible human messengers have to do with the Word which was a verb ("said") in Genesis, a noun (the "word" of *HaShem*) in the Psalms, and a metaphorical personified Word/Wisdom in later Jewish wisdom literature?

Note that saying that Yeshua is the "walking visible" Word (of God) is like saying an individual is "a walking dictionary."

It would be anachronistic to claim that before creation, the historical Yeshua was already born to a Jewish mother and had been raised by Jewish parents and was literally and physically walking around on an earth that had not yet been created.

A Christian responds, "Sir, for you, Yeshua is just a righteous flesh; for me, HE is the Word of God, which existed before the clock ticked."

Again, the personified first-created Word/Wisdom, which was with/next to its Creator, in the beginning, did *not* physically exist as a visible, mortal human creature before it "became flesh." In other words, the Creator's spoken word was later embodied in the life and teachings of Yeshua.

While the personified and invisible (spoken) Word/Wisdom of God existed at the beginning of time, the later visible and historical Jew who embodied the Word/Wisdom in his life and teachings did *not* yet exist.

A Christian responds, "John 17:5 'And now, O Father, glorify thou me with thine own self with the glory which I had with thee before the world was.' Sir, the flesh said it, and I totally agree that the Word became flesh."

In *YoHanan* 17.5, we read, "Now, Father/Creator (please) glorify me (Yeshua) in Your presence (now) with the glory that I (who embodies the firstborn Word) was (destined) to have with You before the world existed." *YoHanan* portrays the historical Yeshua with visible, mortal flesh as embodying the firstborn/first-created Word in his life and teachings. The invisible firstborn spoken Word (*not* the later visible and mortal human creature, Yeshua) was with/next to its Father/Creator "before the world existed." The firstborn/first-created Word became embodied in the life and teachings of the visible, mortal Jewish Yeshua long after God created the world.

The Visible Son, Yeshua, Reveals the Invisible Father/Creator [John 1.18]

The only Creator, the single Source for all that is, "dwells in unapproachable light Whom no human being has ever seen or can see (unlike any visible human creature)." [1 Tim. 6.16]

A Christian responds, "So how does Jesus get away with telling Philip, 'If you have seen me, you have seen the Father'? [John 14.9]"

There is no contradiction between 1 Timothy 6.16 and John 14.9, as some might suppose. Instead, these two passages taken together are simply another way of saying, "No man has ever seen God [the sole Creator]. The unique [and especially-loved] son (Yeshua), the one being in the bosom of the Father (i.e., one who lives in harmony with his Creator's will) that one has declared/revealed [Him]." [John 1.18] Those who have seen or heard the unique son, Yeshua, have perceived or understood the Creator/Father Who sent him. In other words, the Creator declares or reveals Himself through or by the human son, Yeshua, who was created in His image/form like Adam and all other human sons or descendants of Adam.

Another Christian counters with his version, "[John 1:18] ISV 'No one has ever seen God. The unique God, who is close to the Father's side, has revealed him.'"

There are four major textual variants for John 1.18. The most probable original text was "ὁ μονογενὴς υἱός (*ho monogenays uios*) meaning "the unique son," which makes sense in this context and accords with John's usage elsewhere. (cf. John 3.16, 18; 1 John 4.9) However, ὁ μονογενὴς θεὸς (*ho monogenays Theos*) meaning "the unique God" is the most improbable variant. It is unparalleled in John's writings and makes no sense in the context of John 1.18. John had just said at the beginning of the verse, "No one has ever seen *God*," so referring to Yeshua (a human creature which many had seen) as "the unique God" in the next part of the verse cannot be accurate. Also, John goes on to speak of Yeshua in John 1.18 as the unique son (the human being who lives in

harmony with the will of His Father/Creator); that one has revealed the unseen *God*.

https://www.youtube.com/watch?v=W_BGX28er9Y&fbclid
=IwAR1Y8yFc45GSAozAps_vH8hWYP039FneAZ5aQ9iqT
rsJ4_ymu4uW7MBang4

"...The Unique (Especially Loved) Son, the One Who Being/Is (ὁ ὢν *ho on*) in the Bosom/Lap of His Father/Creator..." [John 1.18]

A Christian states, "'o ων' is the son in John 1,18 'Θεὸν οὐδεὶς ἑώρακε πώποτε· ὁ μονογενὴς υἱὸς ὁ ὢν εἰς τὸν κόλπον τοῦ πατρός, ἐκεῖνος ἐξηγήσατο.'"

In John 1.18, we read, "No one has ever seen God (the Father/Creator). The unique (especially loved) son, the one who being/is (ὁ ὢν *ho on*) in the bosom/lap of his Father/Creator, that one made Him (God, the Father/Creator) known." In other words, the unique, especially loved son who lives in harmony with the will of his Father/Creator has reported, interpreted, explained, or revealed the Father's character/will.

A Christian responds, "because he is 'o ων' AS IT SAYS IN JOHN 1:18 meaning GOD."

No, JOHN 1.18 says that "the unique son" is "the one who being/is (ὁ ὢν *ho on*) in the bosom/lap of the Father/Creator (his GOD)." One should not take a couple of Greek words (ὁ ὢν *ho on*), meaning "the one who is," out of their context, and claim it means something unrelated to the way it is used in the verse. In 1 Kings 16.22 (LXX), for example, we read, "ὁ λαὸς ὁ ὢν ὀπίσω Αμβρι (the people who followed *Omree*) ..." The Greek words (ὁ ὢν *ho on*) used to translate this Hebrew verse identify which people are involved: the ones who followed *Omree*/Αμβρι.

The Instruction/*Torah*/Law and Yeshua as Two Sides of the Same Coin

The written Instruction/*Torah* of *HaShem* and the human Yeshua who embodies the Instruction/*Torah* in his life, works, and teachings are two sides of the same coin. One group proclaims the head's side (the personal, Messianic side) of this coin while rejecting the content of his message or meaning on the tail's side (the *Torah* side) of the coin. Another group lives by the *Torah* side of the coin while hiding their faces from the *Torah* man on the 'heads' (Messianic) side of the coin.

HaShem's *Torah* gives content and meaning to the life and teachings of Messiah, Yeshua, as Paul explains, "...the Messiah (Yeshua who embodies the life and teachings of the Instruction/*Torah*/Law) is the actualized goal/purpose (τέλος *telos*) of the *Torah*." [Rom. 10.4-11] Also, Paul writes regarding the hope that "...the Messiah (the way, the truth, and the life of the *Torah* embodied in Yeshua) will be formed in you." [Gal. 4.19]

Note that many years before Paul's writings regarding the *Torah* and the Messiah Yeshua relationship, the prophet Jeremiah predicted, "... 'this is the covenant I (*HaShem*) will make with the people of Israel...,' declares the LORD. 'I will put My Law (i.e., Instruction/*Torah* as modeled by Yeshua in his life and teachings) in their minds and write it on their hearts. I (*HaShem*) will be their God, and they will be my people.'" [Jeremiah 31.33]

Because John claims that Yeshua *ben Yoseph*, the patrilineal son of David, embodies the (spoken) Word/Wisdom or Instruction/*Torah*/Law in his life and teachings, he says in John 1.14 that "the Word (figuratively) became flesh." Therefore, those Christians who reject the Instruction/*Torah*/Law of *HaShem* reject Yeshua as their King/Lord, whether they realize it or not. Also, if Yeshua is the *Torah*-man, then those Jews who accept *HaShem's* Instruction/*Torah*/Law and endeavor to live by it, accept Yeshua as their human Lord or King, whether they realize it or not.

The Messiah Yeshua = the *Torah* Way of Truth and Life

A Christian questions, "Jesus said, 'I am the Way, the Truth, and the Life. No man comes to the Father except through me' John 14:6. Was that a lie or a misquote or the truth? Jesus was either a liar, a crazy man, or you must honor him in order to get to the Father. Which is it?"

Note that King David and many servants of God before and after him faithfully trusted and obeyed the Instruction/*Torah*/Law (i.e., the way, the truth, and the life) of the Father/Creator without ever hearing or knowing about the historical Yeshua of Nazareth. However, because the subservient and faithfully obedient Messiah Yeshua embodies the Instruction/*Torah*/Law in his life and teachings, he can claim metaphorically, "I am the Way, the Truth, and the Life. No one comes to the Father/Creator except through me (the Way, the Truth, and the Life of the *Torah* embodied in the life and teachings of Yeshua)." [John 14.6; cf. Psa. 18.30; 119.30; Prov. 3.18; 4.13; 6.23; 13.8, 14; etc.]

The Jewish Messiah Yeshua fulfills/obeys *HaShem*'s Instruction/*Torah* and encourages his disciples to do the same. However, the imaginary "Christian" god-man "Jesus" allegedly teaches that he terminated *HaShem*'s *Torah* with his death, making the old covenant Law "no longer in effect." Therefore, one should follow a brand-new covenant without being bound by the "old" Law of Moses.

On the other hand, *YoHanan* (John) portrays *HaShem*'s perfect Instruction/*Torah*/Law as being embodied in the life and teachings of Yeshua. This *Torah*-true Jew or ben (son of) *Torah* demonstrates how one should live according to every word that comes from God's mouth. [Matt. 4.4] In other words, like Messiah Yeshua, God's people should embody *HaShem*'s perfect *Torah*/Law (the way, the truth, and the life) in their everyday lives. [cf. Col. 1.27]

A Christian responds, "If the Law were a 'perfect Instruction,' then there would be no need for Christ. But if the law is not a perfect instruction, then it is ineffective to that extent. The Word was made flesh so that the love of God's Word (*Torah*) has been replaced with the love of a person, namely Yeshua *HaMashiach* (or Jesus Christ, for those who don't speak Hebrew)."

There are Jewish Scriptures that support the idea that *HaShem's* Instruction/*Torah*/Law, the expression of the

Father/Creator's will, is "perfect," as we read in the following verses:

"The *Torah* of *HaShem* is perfect, reviving the soul; the decrees of *HaShem* are trustworthy, making wise the simple...." [Psalm 19:7-11]

"But the person who looks into the *perfect* Law, the *Torah* of freedom, and abides by it, not becoming a forgetful hearer but becoming an effectual doer [of this Law], this person will be blessed (rewarded) in his doing." [*Yaakov* (James) 1.25; cf. Acts 22.3]

Without *HaShem's* perfect Instruction/*Torah*/Law, no one would be able to know what "righteousness" is, much less appreciate anyone's devotion to righteousness. In other words, the *Torah* identifies not only *HaShem's* righteous Messiah Yeshua but also all of His righteous people. Since Yeshua taught and lived God's Instruction/*Torah*/Law, he upholds and establishes (i.e., activates and implements rather than replaces) *HaShem's Torah*. Again, Yeshua, the *Torah*-true Jew, demonstrates how one should live according to every word that comes from God's mouth. (Matthew 4.4) He is a human expression of God's *Torah* (not its foreign replacement).

===

A Christian claims, "Jesus is not just some good teacher running around giving His views on God."

Yeshua is *HaShem*'s anointed human king and "the prophet" (a human servant) sent by God to teach and to model obedience to God's Word or Instruction. [cf. Jn. 5.30; 17.8; 20.21]

A Christian responds, "Yes. And more. He is *Torah* incarnate."

Portraying Yeshua as "*Torah* incarnate" is functionally equivalent in meaning to saying he was "the Prophet" sent to model God's Instruction/Word.

A Christian questions, "Really? Would you call Moses 'Torah incarnate'? Elijah? Isaiah?"

Yes! Moses, Elijah, and Isaiah were all prophets sent by *HaShem* not only to give us His word but also to live out His word in their lives. So, Philo taught, God "sends His own words or messengers...." As he also explains, the Creator's Word is "His chief messenger." [Heres 2-5] Philo also refers to Abraham as "the model of Wisdom." [On Dreams I. 69-70] And he describes Moses as "the law-giving Word." [Migr. 23f; cf. 122] But, the personified Word is distinct from its Creator even as the messenger (the one sent) is separate from the Sender.

The people of God are called out to be "the way," "the truth," "the life," and "the light" for others around them. [cf. Ps. 86.11; 119.30; Matt. 5.14-16; John 9.5; 14.6] As the *Baal Shem Tov* remarks, "The whole purpose of the *Torah* is so that man would become a living *Torah*." While Yeshua is the vine, his followers are the branches. [John 15. 1-5; cf. 1 Cor. 3.9] Also, while Yeshua is appointed heir of all, we are also heirs of God...and joint-heirs of the Messiah. [Hebrews 1.2; Romans 8.17-18; Colossians 1.12]

The Most-High God, the Father/Creator, Who *Gives* Us His Word/*Torah*

A Christian says, "I see the Lord Jesus as God--the one who *gave* the *Torah*."

YoHanan (John) teaches us that the personified Word (*Torah*) was beside/next to *the* God/Sovereign Power, Who brought it forth in the beginning and later sent it to us. Even though this firstborn Word was given the title of "God/Power," this secondary "God" was not the Creator Himself, but rather the subservient instrument/agent of its Creator. [cf. Jn. 1.1-3] The Word (who was *of* or *from the* Most High God Whom it was next to in the beginning) became flesh in the sense that it became embodied in the life and teachings of Yeshua. In other words, the human person (creature) whom our eyes have seen and our hands have touched represents the Word of the one God, the single Creator, Whom no one has ever seen or can see. [cf. Jn. 1.18] Also, keep in mind that the Father/Creator's firstborn, first-created Word is NOT the Giver nor the Sender; instead, it is the *given* son or the *sent* Word.

While Jewish authors consistently picture Yeshua as the human prophet/ambassador, and as the priest/mediator and as the metaphorical "son" *of* the Most High God, they never equate him with the Most High God Himself. [1 Tim. 2.5; Lk. 1.76] For example, in Hebrews 1.3 and 3.1 Yeshua is called "the apostle (שליח *shaleeaH* = one sent or an ambassador = τὸν ἀπόστολον *ton apostolon*) and the ruling high priest (הכּהן הגּדֹל *hakohen hagadol* = ἀρχιερέα) of our confession." However, he is *not* "the Majesty on High," Whom he worships and serves.

The "Son" Embodies *HaShem*'s Instruction, Word, Law

What does Yeshua mean in *YoHanan* (John) 3.36 when he says, "He who believes in the son has eternal life, but he who does not obey the son will not see life but must endure God's wrath"? Who or what is "the son" one must believe in or obey in order to participate in eternal life? The "son," one must believe in is Yeshua, who embodies the Instruction/*Torah*/Law in his life and teachings. That is why *YoHanan* (John) characterizes Yeshua metaphorically as one who embodies God's personified first-born "son" or first-created Word/Wisdom, which became embodied in Yeshua's life and teachings. [John 1.1-5; 1.14]

Besides depicting Yeshua as "the son" who embodies *HaShem*'s Word/Wisdom, *Yohanan* also pictures him as "the true light" and as "the way, the truth, and the life," and as "the bread of life." These metaphors are ways of characterizing Yeshua as the one who embodies *HaShem*'s Word/Wisdom or Instruction/T*orah*/Law in his life and teachings. [John 1.9; 6.35; 14.6] So, those who faithfully believe or obey "the son," which is the Instruction/*Torah*/Law embodied in Yeshua, receive eternal life; while those who disbelieve or disobey *HaShem*'s Instruction/*Torah*/Law modeled by Yeshua will not see life.

Note that those who accept the counterfeit Christ/anti-Christ, the alleged God-man or lawless one who leads people away from *HaShem*'s *Torah*, are thereby rejecting the way, the truth, and the life of the genuine *Torah*-man of God. To obey or actively believe in the *Torah*-true son, Yeshua, one must reject the counterfeit Messiah, the lawless "son," who is the anti-Christ, who comes in his own co-equal, co-eternal name. [cf. Jn. 5.43]

In the Jewish Scriptures, both "the son," the historical Yeshua, and the firstborn, first-created Word/Wisdom or the Instruction/*Torah*/Law" are two sides of the same coin. One cannot have "tails" without "heads." If one rejects or ignores *HaShem's* "*Torah*" (tails), he rejects and disobeys the *Torah*-true "son" Yeshua (heads) whether he realizes it or not. Furthermore, if one accepts and obeys *HaShem*'s "*Torah*," he accepts *HaShem*'s "son" Yeshua whether or not one can see the other side of the coin.

"A Person Cannot Receive Anything Unless It is *Given* to Him from Heaven/God" [John 3.27]

The God of Israel, the single Creator, is "the only one having immortality (unlike any slain human creature)." [cf. 1 Tim. 6.15-16]

A Christian responds, "Really? Then how did Jesus raise Himself from the dead?"

The fact that Yeshua died demonstrates that he was mortal rather than immortal. Although God enabled and empowered him to rise from the dead, Yeshua informs us that he does *nothing* on his own authority or power. [cf. John 5.30; 8.28] As Yeshua taught his disciples, "A person cannot receive anything unless it is *given* to him from Heaven/God." [John 3.27] And, Yeshua teaches us that it is the Father Who has *given* all things into his son's hand. [John 3.35; 13.3; 17.7] So, the only way that Yeshua could rise from the dead would be if "he was raised [by his

Creator] from the dead." [John 2.22; 21.14] As we read consistently in the Renewed Covenant Scriptures, "God *raised* him (Yeshua) from the dead." [Act 4.10; cf. Acts 3.26; 13.30; Rom. 7.4; 10.9; Gal. 1.1; Col. 2.12; 1 Peter 1.21]

"…All May Honor the Son, Even As They Honor the Father…" [John 5.22-23]

A Christian claims, "Jesus instructed all men to worship him as God. John 5:23 'That all men should honor the Son, even as they honor the Father. He that honoureth, not the Son honoureth, not the Father which hath sent him.'"

First, it should be noted that honoring someone is not the same as worshiping that person. While we are also commanded to honor or highly respect our parents, it does not mean that we should worship them as being God, the Father/Creator.

Since the finite human son/creature, Yeshua, *represents* the Father/Creator Who sent him, we honor/respect him as we should honor/respect a prophet who represents the Father/Creator. Consequently, in John 3.19, we read, "The son can do nothing of himself." [cf. John 3.30] Nevertheless, the Father/Creator sent/empowered His firstborn son and gave/delegated all judgment to the son who embodies His Instruction/Word in his life and teachings. Again, since the Son represents His Father/Creator, everyone should honor/ respect the Son as they honor/respect the Father Who sent him. [John 3.22-23, 26-27]

Keep in mind that "a person's agent is as himself (שְׁלוּחוֹ שֶׁל אָדָם כְּמוֹתוֹ *Sh'luho shel adam k'moto*)." [*BerakHot* 34B] In other words, "the one who is sent is as the one who sent him." According to this Biblical/Jewish law of agency (שְׁלִיחוּת *shleeHoot*), the human ambassador who represents the King can be addressed *as if* he were the King and he should be respected/honored *as if* he were the One Who sent/empowered him. Since Yeshua was sent/empowered by his God and given/delegated judgment, he should be honored and respected as the Father/Creator's human representative.

People Should Respect the Son, Yeshua, Just As They Respect the Father/Creator [John 5.19-27]

Someone asks, "How do we honor the Messiah just as we honor the Father?"

We honor the Messiah, *HaShem*'s human representative, who embodies the (spoken) Word/Wisdom (Instruction or Law) by following his model of faithful obedience to his Father/Creator. In John 5.19-27, we read, "Then Jesus answered and said to them (some Jews), 'Most assuredly, I say to you, the son (Yeshua) can do *nothing* of himself, but what he sees the Father do; for whatever He does, the son also does in like manner. For the Father loves the son and shows him all things that He Himself does...For the Father judges no one but has committed all judgment to the son (Yeshua who embodies the Instruction/*Torah*), in order that all should respect the son (Yeshua) just as they respect the Father. He who does not respect the Son (Yeshua) does not respect/honor the Father Who sent him....' " In other words, by respecting the Messiah Yeshua (who embodies the Word or Instruction/*Torah*), we respect the Father/Creator Who sent/appointed Yeshua and empowered him to model the Word or Instruction/*Torah*.

"For I (the Bread of Life) Have Not Come Down from Heaven/God to Do My Will..." [John 6.38]

A Christian claims, "Yeshua existed before he was created in the womb [Abba (the Father) creates within the womb - Ps 139:13, Job 31:15]. Before Yeshua was 'created in the womb, ' he existed in the heavens as one of the 'Creator's heavenly agents.'"

John portrays Yeshua *ben Yoseph* as the embodiment of the firstborn (personified spoken) Word, the instrument or means by which the single Creator made all things in the beginning. While the abstract (personified, non-human) Word was with its Creator in the beginning, Yeshua, the later visible human embodiment of that Word, did not yet exist. Also, no author of the Renewed Covenant writings teaches that Yeshua, who was conceived and born at the time of King Herod, existed as one of the Creator's heavenly agents before God created him in the womb.

A Christian responds, "Yeshua spoke for himself concerning where he came from and from who's presence he left. Why do we need verification from other sources? .... *Yohanan* 6:38, 42 Yeshua himself said, 'I have come down from *Shamayim*

(Heaven) not that I may do my *ratzon* (will), but the *ratzon* of the One having sent me.' .... And those of *Yehudah* were saying, 'Is this man not *Yehoshua*/Yeshua [Zech. 6:11-12; Ezra 3:8] *Ben Yosef* [*Ben Dovid*], and do we not know his *Av* (father) and his *Em* (mother)? Now how does he say, 'Out of *Shamayim* I have come down.' [*Yochanan* 1:1,14, *Yohanan* 17:11-12.]"

In *YoHanan* 6.38, 42, Yeshua says, "For I (the embodiment of the bread of life = *HaShem*'s Instruction/Word) have not come down from Heaven/God to do my will but the will of the One Who sent me." [cf. *YoHanan* 6.35, 47-48, 51] Some Jews then ask, "...How can he (Yeshua) say, 'I have come from heaven?'" One should keep in mind that every prophet that is sent by the Father/Creator comes down from Heaven/God to speak God's Word and to do His will. No prophet (who is God's human agent) sent by Heaven comes to do his own will, but the will of the One Who sent him. [*YoHanan* 1.6]

Yeshua claims that God, the Father/Creator, sent him as He sent other prophets before him. Again, every human prophet sent down from Heaven/God carries and delivers God's word for His people to hear. For example, when we read in *YoHanan* 1.6, "There was a man sent from God whose name was John," it means that God delegated him and sent him on a mission to say and do as he was instructed to say and do.

Also, note that as early as the book of Deuteronomy, Moses uses manna, the bread from Heaven, to symbolize God's Instruction/Word. As we read in Deuteronomy 8.2-3, "Remember the (long) way that *HaShem* (ה-ו-ה-י), your God has made you travel in the wilderness these past forty years, that He might test you by hardships to learn what was in your hearts/minds; whether you would keep His commandments or not. He (God) humbled/subjected you to the hardship of hunger. He then fed you with manna (i.e., bread from Heaven), which neither you nor your fathers had ever known, in order to teach you that man does not live on the bread alone, but that man lives by every word that proceeds out of the mouth of *HaShem* (ה-ו-ה-י)." In other words, humankind lives by whatever *HaShem* decrees in His Instruction/Word, which descends from God/Heaven.

Hundreds of years later, the book of John portrays Yeshua throughout his life and teachings as an embodiment of the bread of life, the Instruction or Word (*Logos/Memra*) of God, which Heaven sends down to His people, Israel. So, in *YoHanan* 6.38, we read, "For I (the embodiment of the bread of life = *HaShem*'s Instruction/Word) have not come down (as the nourishing bread of life) from Heaven/God to do my will but the will of the One Who sent me." [cf. *YoHanan* 6.35, 47-48, 51] All who follow in Yeshua's footsteps should also become **the bread of life sent down by** God/Heaven to those around them. As the *Baal Shem Tov* remarks, "The whole purpose of the *Torah* (*HaShem*'s Instruction/Word) is so that a person would become a living *Torah*."

"...Abraham Rejoiced to Foresee My Day" [John 8.56-58]

"...Abraham rejoiced to foresee my (Yeshua's) day (by faith) ... (cf. Heb. 11.8-11) Before Abraham existed, I am he (the embodiment of the firstborn Word = the Son of Man = the promised, foreseen Messiah). [John 8.56-58]

Someone asks, "How does this prove or disprove Yeshua's eternal or non-eternal nature?"

There is no mention of "eternal" found in the claim that Yeshua is the foreseen "Son of Man/Adam," the firstborn among many siblings.

Someone asks, "Help me. How can Yeshua 'be' before Abraham existed? As an idea, maybe? An idea that existed before Abraham?"

Yes, the Messiah "existed in God's thoughts even before the world was created." As we read in _P'sikta Rabbati_ (פְּסִיקְתָּא רַבָּתִי), _Piska_ 33.6, "You find that at the very beginning of the creation of the world, the king Messiah had already come into being, for he existed in God's thoughts even before the world was created. Of his existence Scripture says, 'And there came forth a shoot of the stock of Jesse' (Isaiah 11:1) it does not say 'And there shall come forth' but 'And there came forth,' implying that the shoot of the stock of Jesse had already come forth (in God's mind)."

So, also, in _P'sikta Rabbati_, _Piska_ 36.1, we find, "What is meant by 'in your light do we see light?' ...It is the light of the Messiah of which it is said, 'And God saw the light that it was good.' (Genesis 1.4) This verse proves that the Holy One, blessed be He, _contemplated_ the Messiah and his works before the world was created, and then under His throne of glory put away His Messiah until the time of the generation in which he will appear."

Note that these passages do _not_ indicate that the Messiah existed as a visible, historical human person in the beginning. Instead, they mean that God _foreknew_ or _contemplated_ that He would send His Messiah to His people.

"...the Glory, Which I Was to Have from You Before the Cosmos Was [Created]" [John 17.5]

In John 17.5, we read:
καὶ νῦν δόξασόν με σύ, πάτερ, παρὰ σεαυτῷ
And now You glorify me, Father, in Your presence

τῇ δόξῃ ᾗ εἶχον
with the glory which I was to have

πρὸ τοῦ τὸν κόσμον εἶναι παρὰ σοί.
before the cosmos was [in existence] from You.

The Greek verb, translated as "was to have" (*eixon* εἶχον), is imperfect (an ongoing action in the past, which continues into the present), not aorist (a simple one-time completed action in the past). In other words, Yeshua is not requesting glory, which he once had in the past and then lost. Instead, he is requesting the glory/honor, which he was long destined to have even before the cosmos existed. Since Yeshua finished the work (which the Father gave to him to do), he asks his Creator to glorify/honor him now in His presence with the glory that he was destined to have even before the cosmos was created. [John 17.1-5]

"…. Because You (Father) Loved Me (Yeshua) Before the Foundation of the World" [John 17.24]

A Christian writes, "John 17:24 New Revised Standard Version (NRSV) 24 'Father, I desire that those also, whom you have given me, may be with me where I am, to see my glory, which you have given me because you loved me before the foundation of the world.' …Of course, he (Yeshua) was alive and working with the Father before all creation. So was hasatan."

The firstborn (personified) Word was next to its Creator in the beginning. However, the spoken Word (present at creation) was not embodied in Yeshua's life and teachings until much later in human history. While the visible, mortal son of *Yoseph* and *Meeryam* was *not* born and was *not* physically alive and working with the Father before all creation, God foreknew and loved him "before the foundation of the world." [John 17.24] As we read in 1 Peter 1.20, God foreknew/destined Yeshua to be the Messiah (the firstborn among many siblings) "before the foundation of the world." [cf. Romans 8.29]

Likewise, in John 17.1-5, we read that after Yeshua finishes the work (which the Father gives to him to do), he asks his Creator to glorify/honor him now in His presence with the glory that he was destined to have even before the cosmos was created. Also, besides Yeshua, the Father/Creator foreknew and chose many others for obedience to Himself long before they came into this world. [1 Peter 1.1-2]

"My Lord/Master and My God/Powerful Judge!" [John 20.28]

When *T'oma* (Thomas) addresses Yeshua at the end of the book of *YoHanan* (John), he uses "my God" as a synonym for "my Master/Lord." [John 20.21] In the Jewish scriptures, the title of "Master/Lord" is applied to human masters, the appointed Messiah, and also to the Most High *Adonai*, the single Creator. So also, the Hebrew title "*Eloheem*" (Power) has a range of applications from various human judges and human kings to the human king of human kings, the Messiah Yeshua, and to the Supreme Power, the One and Only Father/Creator Who is greater than everyone, including Yeshua. [Jn. 10.29; 14.28]

A Christian responds, "I would be very interested to hear your evidence that 'God' may mean 'judge' as in a human judge."

The Hebrew title "*Eloheem*" refers to the human king in Ps. 45.6-7, where we read, "Your throne, 'God,' (will remain) forever and ever....Therefore, 'God,' your *Eloheem* (God) has anointed you (with the) oil of joy above your companions." One of the human companions is anointed by his God and set apart from his comrades and called "God." (These verses are quoted and applied to Yeshua in Hebrews 1.8-9.) Also, in Ps. 82.1-6, we read, "God (*Eloheem*) presides in the assembly of the great; He gives judgment (in) among the 'Gods' (*Eloheem*)...I said you are 'Gods' (*Eloheem*); you are all sons of the Most High. But you will die like a man, and you will fall like every other ruler (prince)...." The "Gods" referred to in the various passages from Psalms are human judges or rulers. In fact, Yeshua quotes Psalm 82.6 passage in his defense against the false charge of blasphemy in *YoHanan* 10. 31-38.

Human beings are addressed as "Gods/*Eloheem*" in other passages besides those found in the Psalms. For example, in *Shemot* (Exodus) 21.6 we read, "Then his Master (אֲדֹנָיו *Adonav*) must take him before the *Eloheem* (הָאֱלֹהִים the Gods/the Powers that be or the Judges) ..." Many translate "*haEloheem*" in Exodus 21.6 as "the judges" since the context addresses the laws of Hebrew masters and servants. And in *Shemot* (Exodus) 22.7-9, we read, "...the owner of the house must appear before the '*Eloheem*' (the Gods/Powers or the Judges) to determine whether he has laid his hands on the other man's property. ...both parties are to bring their cases before the '*Eloheem*' (the Gods/Powers or Judges)." It is no wonder that we address human judges today as "your honor." [See *B'resheeth* (Genesis) 6.2 and *Shemot* (Exodus) 22.28 for other references for the use of "*Eloheem*" (God/Power) applied to human beings.]

A Christian continues, "Even if 'judge' is within the semantic range of the word 'God,' that is a stretch to limit Thomas' words at a moment of existential realization to "my master and my judge."

Thomas addressed the resurrected Yeshua as "my Master/Lord and my Power/God," meaning my anointed human Lord/King and my appointed God/Power or Judge. Thomas viewed Yeshua as the human Master/Lord of master/lords and the human King of kings and the human Judge of judges. Paul writes that God will "judge the inhabited earth in righteousness by a *man* (Yeshua) whom He (*HaShem*) has designated," he is claiming that Yeshua will eventually be the Creator's appointed human judge. [Acts 17.31]

===

A Christian asks, "In what sense does a human master and judge have the power to raise from the dead?"

In *YoHanan* 5.26 we read that the Father/Creator "*gave* to the son to have life in himself." The Father/Creator who raised Yeshua from the dead *gave* to him "all authority in heaven and on the earth." [Matt. 28.18]

A Christian remarks, "Thomas is expressing awe at his discovery of Yeshua's nature."

Yes, *T'oma* is expressing his awe at his discovery of Yeshua's lordship or rulership over his life by using terms of respect, which were commonly addressed to human kings in the ancient near East.

A Christian writes, "Shmuel, one can find anything in the scriptures that they want to find. The key is to determine what the text is saying, not what we can limit it or stretch it to mean. Scholars call this the difference between reading into the text (eisegesis) and reading from the text (exegesis)."

Understanding and reporting the original cultural and linguistic context of a Jewish text should not be confused with "eisegesis."

The Afflicted Person, the Human Suppliant, Viewed as God's Agent [Psalm 101.25-27; Hebrews 1.10-12]

Someone asks, "Hebrews 1:10-11 …how should we address these verses (to counter the arguments) given by a trinitarian?"

In Hebrews 1.10-11, the author quotes the Greek version of Psalm 101.26-27 instead of the Masoretic Hebrew text. In the Greek version of Psalm 101.23-28, God responds to the prayer of the afflicted person, which is expressed previously in Psalm 101.1-22:

"23) He (God) answered him (the afflicted suppliant) in the way of his strength (saying), 'You (the suppliant) tell Me (God, the Father) the shortness of My days (i.e., you, the suppliant, should acknowledge the shortness of the set time for the restoration of *Tzion* referred to in verse 14). 24) Do not take Me (God, the Father). In other words, you (the suppliant) should not summon Me, the Father) amid My days (i.e., in the middle of the set time for the restoration of *Tzion*). Your (the afflicted suppliant's) years are throughout all generations. 25) In the beginning, you (the suppliant), Master/Lord (i.e., the metaphorical firstborn, first-created Word/Wisdom), laid the foundation of the earth; and the heavens are the works of your hands. 26) They (the earth and the heavens) will perish, but you (the Master/Lord, the metaphorical firstborn, first-created Word/Wisdom) remain…. 27) But, you (the suppliant viewed as Master/Lord or Word/Wisdom) are the same and your years shall not fail. 28) The children of your servants shall dwell (securely), and their seed/offspring shall prosper (or be preserved) forever.'"

Since the quote found in Hebrews 1.10-11 is taken from the Greek version of Psalm 101.25-27, it is quite different from the Hebrew Masoretic text found in Psalm 102.25-28. In the Greek version, when God responds to the afflicted person, He addresses him (the afflicted person) as "Master/Lord." In other words, the afflicted person is viewed as God's *agent*, the firstborn Word who "founded the earth..." In the Greek text, God's subservient and secondary "Master/Lord" is considered to be the embodiment of the firstborn Word/Wisdom by which everything was made.

In contrast to the Greek version of Psalm 101.23-28, where God answers the prayer of an afflicted person, in the Masoretic Hebrew version of Psalm 102.24-29, the afflicted person's prayer to God goes on without a response from God. In other words, the full Hebrew version of Psalm 102 from the beginning to the end is one continuous prayer of the afflicted person to God:

"24) He (the foreign enemy) has sapped/afflicted my (i.e., an afflicted person's) strength on the way. He (the enemy) has shortened my days, 25) I say, 'My God (*Elee* אֵלִי), do not remove me (an afflicted person) amid my days – Your (God's) years endure through all generations. 26) Long ago, You (God) laid the foundations of the earth, and the heavens are the work of Your hands. 27) They (the heavens and the earth) will perish, but You (Father/Creator) will endure…. 28) But You (God) are enduring and Your years will never end. The descendants (children) of Your servants will settle [in the land], and their seed/offspring will be established before You."